Personalisation: a rough guide
(revised edition)

Sarah Carr

Royal College of
Occupational
Therapists

First published in Great Britain in October 2008, updated in
April 2010 by the Social Care Institute for Excellence

© SCIE 2010

ISBN 978-1-904812-48-7

Written by Sarah Carr (Social Care Institute for Excellence)

This report is available in print and online
www.scie.org.uk

Social Care Institute for Excellence
Goldings House
2 Hay's Lane
London SE1 2HB
tel 020 7089 6840
fax 020 7089 6841
textphone 020 7089 6893
www.scie.org.uk

Front cover image kindly supplied by istock

This publication has no connection with Rough Guides Limited – the publisher of travel
guides and various non-reference titles based at 80 Strand, London WC2R 0RL.

Contents

Foreword

Personalisation means thinking about public services and social care and support in an entirely different way – starting with the person rather than the service. It requires the transformation of adult social care.

By identifying and sharing knowledge about good practice, SCIE has a special role to play in the transformation of social care services for adults. We were a signatory to the Putting People First concordat which set out our shared commitment to finding new ways to improve adult social care in England.

This newly revised version of our very popular 2008 guide is intended to update people on the latest about the implementation and understanding of care and support. For example, since 2008 significant developments have occurred in relation to the social care workforce and in social care regulation; more is known about personal budgets, commissioning and the role of the independent sector. We've tried to capture some of the key developments, evidence and information in this new version of the guide. SCIE continues to help the sector by rapidly absorbing lessons from innovations and pilots, by listening to users and carers and by drawing on the experiences of those in practice, policy and research. We offer an expanding range of resources designed to support everyone on their personalisation journey, including Social Care TV, and e-learning – products which are easy to find and use.

We have had help from a wide variety of people and hope that you find this new version of the guide a useful contribution to making personalisation a reality.

Julie Jones CBE, Chief Executive, SCIE

Acknowledgements

Special thanks to Richard Humphries for his invaluable expert advice and editorial input.

Many thanks also go to Rachel Dittrich, Hampshire County Council Adult Services Department, for her contributions to the first (October 2008) edition of this book.

Thanks to all those who submitted practice examples, especially:

- Sara Lewis, Practice Development Manager, SCIE
- Mike Rudd, Project Support Officer, Strategic Development Unit, Adult and Community Services, Lancashire County Council
- Faith Dawes, Senior Communications Officer, Anchor Trust
- Jacqui London, Access Point Manager, Brighton and Hove City Council
- Karen Elsbury, Area Manager, Sense East
- Naz Khan, Link Team and Language Shop Manager, Oldham Council
- Richard Watts, Policy Director, Essex Coalition of Disabled People (ECDP).

Finally thanks to everyone at the SCIE Partners' Council and the personalisation project team who helped shape the original idea for the guide.

Introduction

Photo: istock

I just want to control my own life ... I like to socialise with other people and meet new friends. I just want to enjoy my freedom. I don't want people to control my life for me I want to control it myself. That's what my Mum brought me up for to control my own life. ('Maria' in Taylor and others, 2007, p 92)

Personalisation means, for me, that I want to be able to stay living in my own home. I want to be able to access every kind of public transport. I guess it's really about the ordinary, to be honest. (Anne McFarlane in Social Care TV: Personalisation for older people living at home).

Public service reform has proceeded far more successfully where government has successfully articulated a story about reform ... that has engaged the workforce. (Brooks, 2007, p 13)

This publication aims to tell the story so far about the personalisation of adult social care services. It is intended to be a 'rough guide', exploring what personalisation is, where the idea came from and placing the transformation of adult social care in the wider public service reform agenda. It explains some of the basics and examines what personalisation means for different social care stakeholders and for the sector as a whole.

Who the guide is aimed at
This guide is aimed at frontline practitioners and first-line managers in statutory and independent sector social care services.

How SCIE is trying to help
By identifying and transferring knowledge about good practice, SCIE has a special role to play in the transformation of social care services for adults. The organisation's priorities for 2008–11 will:

- support the transformation of social care services to enable people to lead full and independent lives
- support the delivery of services to transform the lives of families and their children
- raise the status of social care through a workforce that learns and innovates.

SCIE was a signatory to the Putting People First (HM Government, 2007) concordat, which set out the shared commitment to the transformation of adult social care in England. It is also a member of the Transforming Adult Social Care Programme Board and Delivery Coordination Group.

SCIE recognises that the concept of personalisation continues to evolve in terms of both policy and practice. It has produced further materials that reflect the evidence and experience arising from implementation and further developments. This guide is not an effort to capture everything that is happening in personalisation, but rather offers a brief, accessible overview of some of the ideas, issues and implications.

The basics

What is personalisation?

Personalisation means thinking about care and support services in an entirely different way. This means starting with the person as an individual with strengths, preferences and aspirations and putting them at the centre of the process of identifying their needs and making choices about how and when they are supported to live their lives. It requires a significant transformation of adult social care so that all systems, processes, staff and services are geared up to put people first.

The traditional service-led approach has often meant that people have not received the right help at the right time and have been unable to shape the kind of support they need. Personalisation is about giving people much more choice and control over their lives and goes well beyond simply giving personal budgets to people eligible for council funding. Personalisation means addressing the needs and aspirations of whole communities to ensure everyone has access to the right information, advice and advocacy to make good decisions about the support they need. It means ensuring that people have wider choice in how their needs are met and are able to access universal services such as transport, leisure and education, housing, health and opportunities for employment, regardless of age or disability.

Personalisation means:

- tailoring support to people's individual needs
- ensuring that people have access to information, advocacy and advice to make informed decisions about their care and support

- finding new collaborative ways of working (sometimes known as co-production) that support people to actively engage in the design, delivery and evaluation of services
- developing local partnerships to co-produce a range of services for people to choose from and opportunities for social inclusion and community development
- developing the right leadership and organisational systems to enable staff to work in creative, person-centred ways
- embedding early intervention, re-ablement and prevention so that people are supported early on and in a way that's right for them
- recognising and supporting carers in their role, while enabling them to maintain a life beyond their caring responsibilities
- ensuring all citizens have access to universal community services and resources – a total system response.

The Department of Health (DH) makes it clear that: 'Importantly, the ability to make choices about how people live their lives should not be restricted to those who live in their own homes. It is about better support, more tailored to individual choices and preferences in all care settings' (DH, 2008a, p 5). This has equal, if not more, resonance for those living in residential care homes and other institutions, where personalised approaches may be less developed. Here, the independent sector has a crucial role to play in delivering personalised solutions for people no longer living in their own homes.

Personalisation is a relatively new term and there are different ideas about what it could mean and how it will work in practice. There are several terms used in association with personalisation or to describe services or activities that reflect the agenda. Some terms are used interchangeably and others are used in relation to particular policies, processes or people who use services. Based on our current understanding, the list below aims at clarifying some of the different examples of personalised approaches:

- **Person-centred planning** was an approach formally introduced in the 2001 *Valuing people* strategy (DH, 2001) for people with learning disabilities. The person-centred planning approach has similar aims and elements to personalisation, with a focus on supporting individuals to live as independently as possible, have choice and control over the services they use and to access both wider public and community services and employment and education. Rather than fitting people to services, services should fit the person.

Photo: Careimages.com

- **Person-centred care** has the same meaning as person-centred planning, but is more commonly used in the field of dementia care and services for older people.
- **Person-centred support** is a term being used by some service user groups to describe personalisation.
- **Independent living** is one of the goals of personalisation. It does not mean living on your own or doing things alone, but rather it means 'having choice and control over the assistance and/or equipment needed to go about your daily life; having equal access to housing, transport and mobility, health, employment and education and training opportunities' (Office for Disability Issues, 2008, p 11).
- **Self-directed support** is a term that originated with the in Control project and relates to a variety of approaches to creating personalised social care. in Control sees self-directed support as the route to achieving independent living. It says that the defining characteristics of self-directed support are:
  - the support is controlled by the individual
  - the level of support is agreed in a fair, open and flexible way

- any additional help needed to plan, specify and find support should be provided by people who are as close to the individual as possible
- the individual should control the financial resources for their support in a way they choose
- all of the practices should be carried out in accordance with an agreed set of ethical principles. (Adapted from Duffy, 2008.)

More about self-directed support

Self-directed support is the mechanism and framework through which personal budgets are being delivered. The Department of Health along with key local authority social care stakeholders have worked on defining what self-directed support is and how it is to be implemented. They say:

Self-directed support involves finding out what is important to people with social care needs and their families and friends, and helping them to plan how to use the available money to achieve these aims. It is about focusing on outcomes and ensuring that people have choice and control over their support arrangements. In practice, implementing self-directed support in social care means ensuring the following elements are in place:

- **Self-directed assessment:** simplified assessment that is led as far as possible by the person, in partnership with the professional and focuses on the outcomes that they want to achieve in meeting their eligible needs. Assessment looks at the individual's circumstances and whole situation and takes account of the situation and needs of carers, family members and others who provide informal support. The council's duty to assess needs can be met through proportionate self-directed assessment and support planning processes, and the council is legally responsible for signing off the assessment and support plan.

- **Up-front (indicative) allocation:** The person has a clear indication at an early stage of the amount of council money (if any) that is likely to be available to achieve these outcomes before support planning takes place. This amount may be adjusted following the development of the support plan.
- **Support planning:** There is advice and support available to help people (no matter where their money comes from) to develop plans that will achieve a desired set of outcomes. Putting People First local government consortium has said that the plan should be 'proportionate and non-prescriptive' – it need not be expressed in units of provision (like hours of care) and can include broader needs and desired outcomes beyond the needs that made the person eligible for support (Putting People First consortium, 2010a). Arrangements should make the most use of any existing social support networks and mainstream services. For those people who will be receiving ongoing council funding (i.e. with a personal budget) to meet their care and support costs, the council must sign off support plans to ensure that eligible needs will be met and any risks managed.
- **Choice and control:** the person should (as far as capacity allows) decide how any council funding should be managed and decide how best to spend it to meet their needs to achieve their agreed outcomes. Decisions should not be constrained by the menu of services currently offered. Councils should not require personal budgets and support plans to be expressed in terms of 'hours of support'. This could reduce flexibility and result in service-led solutions.
- **Review:** The council should have a process for checking whether the outcomes agreed in the support plan are being achieved (adapted from ADASS, 2009a, pp 3–4.)

They continue:

The move towards self-directed support and personal budgets involves comprehensive change – the policy makes it clear self-directed support needs to become the core way of doing business. It is not an 'option'. Implementing self-directed support is as much about changing culture as about changing systems' (ADASS, 2009a, p 5).

This section addresses some of the questions that people have asked about the different approaches to delivering personalised social care.

What is a personal budget?

In December 2007, *Putting people first* (HM Government, 2007) proposed that all social care users should have access to a personal budget, with the intention that they can use it to exercise choice and control to meet their agreed social care outcomes. In March 2009 the Association of Directors of Adult Social Services (ADASS) reported that 93,000 people were receiving personal budgets (including direct payments) (ADASS, 2009b). The Care Quality Commission (CQC) reported in February 2010 that 115,000 adults over 18 in England were receiving a personal budget or direct payment option, which represents 6.5 per cent of all adults using services in 2008/9 (CQC, 2010). The government expect all 152 councils in England to have made significant steps towards transforming their adult social care services, including having at least 30 per cent of eligible adults on a personal budget, by 2011, with access to information and advice services to support them (and also to support those using their own money to buy care and support).

Personal budgets have been informed both by the experience of direct payments and also by the piloting of individual budgets in 13 English local authorities in 2007–08.

Individual budgets attempted to combine the following funding streams:

- local authority adult social care
- integrated community equipment services
- Disabled Facilities Grants
- Supporting People for housing-related support
- Access to Work
- Independent Living Fund.

Research into the effectiveness of the pilot schemes was conducted by the Individual Budgets Evaluation Network (IBSEN) (Glendinning and others, 2008). The evaluation was promising and showed that people can benefit from having more choice and control over their social care and support services as well as indicating that this could cost no more than traditional services.

However, the research also showed that integrating these funding streams together could not happen without central government changes to some of the legislation and administration rules relating to some of the different funds. The government is currently focusing on using only social care money in the immediate future – this is known as a personal budget. The Department of Health has said that the term individual budget is no longer in use and that the correct term for allocation of social care funding to an eligible adult through self-directed support is personal budget (ADASS, 2009a).

Key to the personal budget approach is giving clear, early understanding of the amount available to the individual, so that they can influence or control how it is spent, in a way which helps them best meet their needs. A personal budget should focus on providing for on-going support and care needs, and should normally be considered only after examination of relevant preventative and re-ablement options (ADASS, 2009a). Personal budgets must be implemented within the framework of self-directed support which involves self-directed assessment; 'up-front' allocation of funds and support planning to promote maximum choice and control (ibid). They are not a crisis intervention option.

ADASS, together with the Department of Health, have issued some useful information about how personalisation, including personal budgets, can be implemented within the current social care legal framework, including the duty of the local authority to assess people in need of social care and support and the right to a direct payment for eligible individuals (ADASS, 2009c).

Several forms of Resource Allocation System (RAS) are in use around the country to determine the size of the personal budget. The majority of these systems are points-based, offering transparency, so that the individual knows at an early stage what resources are available to them in their personal budget allocation (ADASS, 2009d). In this way, outcomes defined by the person using the service drive the spending. This allocation can be either a full or a partial contribution to social care costs. The person may also choose to pay for additional support on top of the budget. A personal budget may be taken by an eligible person:

- in the form of a direct (cash) payment, held directly by the person or, where they lack capacity, by a 'suitable person'
- by way of an 'account' held and managed by the council in line with the person's wishes, that is to pay for community care services which are commissioned by the council, or as an account placed with a third party (provider) and 'called-off' by the user in direct negotiation with the provider. This 'managed option' includes Individual Service Funds (ISFs) and can be the means by which someone who does not opt for a direct payment can draw on existing or new contracts to suit their needs without taking on direct budget management responsibilities.
- as a mixture of the above
  (Adapted from ADASS, 2009a, p 5.)

What is a direct payment?

A direct payment is a means-tested cash payment made in the place of regular social service provision to an individual who has been assessed as needing support. Following a financial assessment, those eligible can choose to take a direct payment and arrange for their own support instead. The money included in a direct payment only applies to social services. A direct payment is one way of taking a personal budget.

As part of self-directed support, the personal budget holder is encouraged to devise a support plan to help them meet their personal outcomes. Assistance in developing this plan can come from care managers, social workers, independent brokerage agencies and family and friends. Once a plan has been devised support can be purchased from:

- statutory social services
- the private sector
- the voluntary or third sector
- user-led organisations
- community groups
- neighbours, family and friends.

Practice example: Direct payments for lesbian and gay people

The former Commission for Social Care Inspection issued a series of equality and diversity bulletins designed to support providers in addressing the personalisation agenda in social care. The first bulletin looked at providing appropriate services for lesbian, gay, bisexual and transgender people and found that many people valued the choice and control direct payments gave them:

'I am a direct payments user. Yes, it has been a much better option for me as a gay person, no question. I would have been imprisoned with a care agency. Can't stress that too strongly. I live at home supported by people I recruit who I am very clear with who I am. They don't change every week and they are not all straight or gay ... life has been a thousand times better on direct payments, even with its challenges.'

'Staff treated me with respect because I was in control of who was employed and what they did to assist me, both in my home and the wider community. I would not employ someone who decided they would take over my life and decide what was best for me. And I certainly would not employ any person who did not feel comfortable around my lifestyle.'

People can use their budgets to access a wide range of services, including traditional social care, as long as it is legal and meets agreed outcomes.

Personal budgets are a conscious attempt to shift control to consumers. Rather than receiving a fixed range of services and little choice) individuals should be better able to design the services, frequently non-traditional, which best meet their agreed outcomes and agreed care plan. This support plan is periodically reviewed with the person to make sure agreed outcomes are being met and to respond to any changes (Bennett, Cattermole and Sanderson, 2009). Evidence from piloting and early adoption shows that some people will use the new flexibilities to design very different services, whilst others value the ability to adjust more conventional packages to deliver a service more responsive to their own needs (Bartlett, 2009).

More about 'managed' personal budgets

Material from the Department of Health, ADASS, IDeA and LGA (Putting People First consortium, 2010a; Putting People First consortium, 2010b; DH, 2010a) clarifies how local authorities should be implementing the personal budget option for people who do not want a direct payment and would prefer their personal budget to be managed for them. A managed personal budget means either:

- the local authority places an individual's personal budget with a third party so day to day business arrangements are between the service user who has a personal budget and the third party provider (purchasing or commissioning) OR
- the local authority itself holds the personal budget and manages/arranges the services on behalf of the service user (providing in-house owned or managed services).

The managed option should not mean less opportunity for the person using services to exercise choice and control than if they chose to have a direct payment. Whatever the personal budget option, people must know what sum of money is available to them and be offered genuine choice and control over the services provided. Someone who decides to keep existing service arrangements should be making a positive choice, having been provided with all the support and information they require to make the decision. Having made an informed choice about their care and support people using services should:

- receive a regular statement showing how their personal budget has been spent and the remaining balance
- have easy access to support services that encourage them to think about new ways they can use their personal budget flexibly to get the care and support that is most suitable for their needs.

The provision of personal budgets needs to be consistent with the principles and values of personalisation – personal budgets should maximise choice and control for people using services, their carers and families wherever possible. The Department of Health is clear that local authorities should avoid strategies to 'bolster personal budget numbers at the expense of the wider Putting People First agenda...Without changing internal processes and culture, establishing support services, developing markets and altering commissioning contracts it is highly unlikely that real choice and control will be provided' (Putting People First consortium, 2010b, p 8).

Further developments with choice and control in health and welfare

Personal health budgets

In order to extend the principles of personalisation, choice and control into health, and following positive initial outcomes for personal budgets in social care, the NHS is exploring how personal health budgets could work for people with long term conditions, including mental health problems (The NHS Confederation, 2009a). The Department of Health has initiated a national pilot programme of 75 Primary Care Trusts (PCTs) in 68 sites. Twenty of these will have been selected for an in-depth study, as part of a wider evaluation exploring the potential of personal health budgets to benefit different groups of people. The pilot programme will run until 2012 (DH, 2009a). The Department of Health have said that:

A personal health budget makes it clear to someone getting support from the NHS and the people who support them how much money is available for their care and lets them agree the best way to spend it. (Department of Health, 2009b, p 4)

They think personal health budgets could work in three ways:

1 **Notional budget**. No money changes hands. The person knows how much money is available and talks to their doctor or care manager about the different ways to spend that money on meeting their needs. Then the agreed care is arranged.
2 **Real budget held by a third party**. A different organisation or trust holds the money for the person helps them work out their needs and then buys the chosen services.
3 **Direct payment**. The person gets the cash to buy the services they and their doctor or care manager decide they need. The person has to show what they have spent it on, but they buy and manage services themselves.

Options 1 and 2 are possible now. The Department of Health have worked to change the law so that direct payments for healthcare in certain circumstances can be tested. The Health Act – which received Royal Assent on 12 November 2009 – extends these options by allowing selected primary care trust sites to pilot direct payments. There is a government consultation on proposals for regulations and guidance to govern how direct payments would work in practice (Department of Health, 2009a).

However, as with personal budgets in social care, it is thought that if 'employed in isolation from other aspects of personalisation, personal health budgets are likely to have minimal impact on the health system' (NHS Confederation, 2009b, p 2).

Right to Control Trailblazers

The Office for Disability Issues has a goal of achieving equality for disabled people by 2025 and is working with disabled people to explore different ways to reach this goal. The Department for Work and Pensions' White Paper *Raising expectations and increasing support: Reforming welfare for the future* (DWP, 2008) set out proposals for the Right to Control. The Right is about empowering disabled people by giving them greater choice and control over public money currently spent on their behalf. This would put disabled people in charge of deciding how their support needs can be best met. The Office for Disability Issues is going to test how the Right to Control will work for disabled adults in a number of local authority areas in England. These will be called Trailblazer sites and the outcome of the Trailblazers will be used to inform any decisions on wider roll-out (ODI, 2009a).

People were consulted on what support should be in the Trailblazers; how disabled people and their organisations will work to develop the Trailblazers; what support disabled people will need to exercise the Right; what Right to Control means for service providers and support services; and views on cost and viability (ODI, 2009a). A feasibility study was also carried out (Purdon et al, 2009) and a Right to Control prospectus for potential Trailblazers has been published outlining more about the initiative (ODI, 2009b).

Trailblazers will explore how disabled people can exercise greater choice and control over the following funding streams (which will still be governed by the existing criteria):

- Work Choice
- Access to Work
- Independent Living Fund (ILF)
- Disabled Facilties Grant (DFG).

Disabled people taking part in the Trailblazers will have a legal right to:

- be told how much money they are eligible to receive
- have choice and control over the support they receive
- be able to choose how they receive the support
- decide and agree the outcomes they want to achieve based on the objectives of the funding stream with the relevant public body.

Disabled people in Trailblazer sites can carry on having existing services if they are happy with them. They can also have the option to take a cash payment to buy equipment and support services themselves or they can have a combination of arranged support and equipment and a cash payment (ODI, 2009b).

Where has personalisation come from?

Although the term personalisation is relatively recent, it has grown from a number of different ideas and influences that are summarised in this section.

Personalisation originates at least in part from **social work values**. Good social work practice has always involved putting the individual first; values such as respect for the individual and self-determination have long been at the heart of social work. In this sense the underlying philosophy of personalisation is familiar. The British Association of Social Workers (BASW) states that social work is committed to the five basic values of human dignity and worth; social justice; service to humanity, integrity and competence (BASW, 2002).

Photo: istock

In terms of **public policy**, personalisation is not just about social care but is a central feature of the government's agenda for public sector reform. The Prime Minister's Strategy Unit report *Building on progress: Public services* (Prime Minister's Strategy Unit, 2007) described it as: 'the process by which services are tailored to the needs and preferences of citizens. The overall vision is that the state should empower citizens to shape their own lives and the services they receive' (p 33). Personalisation has become a key concept for the future of the NHS (DH, 2008d).

Its application to adult social care was announced in *Putting people first: A shared vision and commitment to the transformation of adult social care* (HM Government, 2007) – a ground-breaking concordat between central government, local government and the social care sector. This officially introduced the idea of a personalised adult social care system, where people will have maximum choice and control over the services they receive. It links to wider cross-government strategy including the notion of local authority 'place-shaping' (Lyons, 2007) and the local government White Paper *Strong and prosperous communities* (Department for Communities and Local Government, 2006).

The New Deal outlined in the 2008 Carers' Strategy has integrated and personalised services at its heart. Carers want recognition of their work and expertise, better service coordination, better information, improved joint working between staff and agencies, health and social care. Like Putting People First, the Carers' Strategy has been agreed by several government departments and was the result of a wide consultation. The shared vision is that by 2018 'carers will be universally recognised and valued as being fundamental to strong families and stable communities. Support will be tailored to meet individuals' needs, enabling carers to maintain a balance between their caring responsibilities and a life outside caring, whilst enabling the person they support to be a full and equal citizen' (HM Government, 2008, p 7).

The 2010 White Paper *Building the National Care Service* (HM Government, 2010) sets out how personalised social care and support can be delivered and funded in the long term through the development of a National Care Service, developed in response to

2009's Big Care Debate. The aim is to build a social care system that is fairer, simpler and more affordable with clear standards and entitlements. The White Paper outlines the following founding principles for the National Care Service:

1 Be universal – supporting all adults with an eligible care need within a framework of national entitlements
2 Be free when people need it – based on need, rather than the ability to pay
3 Work in partnership – with all the different organisations and people who support individuals with care and support needs day-to-day
4 Ensure choice and control – valuing all, treating everyone with dignity, respecting an individual's human rights, personal to every individual's needs and putting people in charge of their lives
5 Support family, carers and community life – recognising the vital contribution families, carers and communities play in enabling people to realise their potential
6 Be accessible – easy to understand, helping people make the right choices. (HM Government, 2010, p 13)

The White Paper emphasises the importance of jointly provided, joined-up, high quality, flexible services to give people active choice and control over their care and support. The National Care Service is based on these six pillars:

1 Prevention and wellbeing services to keep you independent
2 Nationally consistent eligibility criteria for social care enshrined in law
3 A joined-up assessment
4 Information and advice about care and support
5 Personalised care and support, through a personal budget
6 Fair funding, with a collective, shared responsibility for paying for care and support. (ibid, p 14)

Staying with public policy, personalisation can be seen as echoing many of the themes of the **community care reforms** that followed the National Health Service and Community Care Act 1990. The aim of these changes was to develop a needs-led approach, in which new arrangements for assessment and care management would lead to individuals receiving tailored packages of care instead of standard, block-contracted services.

In practical terms, a major impetus behind the development of individual or personal budgets has been the experience of **direct payments** which became available, initially to disabled adults of working age in England, as a result of the Community Care (Direct Payments) Act 1996, and have since been extended to other groups. The popularity and success of direct payments has stimulated much of the thinking around individual and personal budgets.

Significantly, direct payments came about and were championed by disabled people themselves. The **service user movement** and the **social model of disability** have been powerful driving forces.

Practice example
Delivering personalisation to black and minority ethnic communities – Oldham Link Team and Language Shop

So that all citizens benefit from personalised care and support, those responsible for planning and providing services need to take steps to ensure that services are accessible and appropriate for people from a range of diverse backgrounds.

The Oldham Link Team and Language Shop is situated within the local authority and works to promote equal access to social care and support via language and community liaison work with black and minority ethnic (BME) people, focusing particularly on assessment and support planning. The team works at strategic and operational as well as frontline delivery level across adult social care.

The aim is to empower individuals, families and communities by providing relevant accessible information and on-going support to people to get the most from the personal budget option. The team also has a role in developing and strengthening services which take holistic, flexible approaches to support provision which accounts for the family context and cultural needs. This has allowed a wider and more appropriate choice for people from local BME communities and has improved uptake of personal budgets. For instance, one provider can guarantee gender specific support and is able to provide significant flexibility, choice and control to the users of the service who are able to cancel and rearrange scheduled sessions at minimal notice.

The team also works at strategic level with commissioners and service planners within the local authority. As part of their community liaison role, the team can provide intelligence for the strategic commissioning and development of care and support services which are appropriate for the local population. For example, they have recently identified a need for a suitable brokerage service. By offering an analysis of social care assessments which were not successful, the team can potentially identify any patterns and barriers in assessment practice or service provision which may need to be addressed at a strategic level. They have recommended that the assessment process be enhanced by the use of knowledgeable language support workers rather than generic interpreters.

Personalisation has some of its roots in the disability, mental health survivor and service user movements which emerged in the 1970s, where individuals and groups undertook direct action and lobbied for change. Independent living, participation, control, choice and empowerment are key concepts for personalisation and they have their origins in the independent living movement and the social model of disability. The current personalisation policy has been influenced by the practical work of **in Control**, established as a social enterprise in 2003, which has pioneered the use of **self-directed support** and personal budgets as a way to reform the current social care system.

The initial phase of in Control's work was carried out across six local authorities from 2003 to 2005 and focused mainly on people with learning disabilities. It was positively evaluated and led on to a second phase which began to test the model for different people using social care (Poll and others, 2006). The whole evaluation collected information on 196 people in 17 English local authorities. The majority of people reported improvements to their lives since they began using self-directed support (Poll and Duffy, 2008). Now over 100 local authorities are looking towards the in Control self-directed support and personal budget model as a solution to delivering personalised social care services for all adults, and over 3,500 people are directing their own support.

Finally, personalisation has been shaped by the **policy thinking and ideas** of researchers, policy analysts and think tanks. One of the most significant contributors is Charles Leadbeater, whose influential Demos report *Personalisation through participation* (2004b) outlined a potential new script for public services. Drawing heavily on some of the influences highlighted above, he emphasises the direct participation of the people who use services: 'By putting users at the heart of services, by enabling them to become participants in the design and delivery, services will be more effective by mobilising millions of people as co-producers of the public goods they value' (Leadbeater, 2004b, p 19). He argues that personalised public services can have at least five different meanings:

- providing people with customer-friendly versions of existing services
- giving people who use services more say in how they are run, once they have access to them
- giving people who use services a more direct say in how money is spent on services
- turning people who use services into co-designers and co-producers of services
- enabling self-organisation by society (Leadbeater, 2004a, p 1).

The last two meanings are defined as 'deep personalisation', with people who use services working in equal partnership with providers. This is the type of personalisation that underpins social care transformation. It is not about modifying existing services, but changing whole systems and the way people work together.

Wider views of personalisation

Another term being used in discussions about personalisation is 'co-production'. Co-production is a fairly recent term that is used as a new way of talking about direct participation, community involvement and power and expertise sharing in social care services in the UK. It has also been called 'co-creation' or 'co-design', and can be seen as a way of building social capital.

Putting People First asserts that the transformation of adult social care programme 'seeks to be the first public service reform programme which is co-produced, co-developed, co-evaluated and recognises that real change will only be achieved through the participation of users and carers at every stage' (HM Government, 2007, p 1). In proposals for new ways of organising and delivering social care services, people who use services have suggested that 'service user-controlled organisations can be a site where social workers are employed working alongside service users in a hands-on way' (Shaping Our Lives and others, 2007, p 13). This would seem to encapsulate the essence of co-production in adult social care.

Research on co-production has shown that frontline workers should focus on people's abilities rather than seeing them as problems (Boyle and others, 2006) and should have the right skills to do this. It has also said that developing staff confidence and improving how they feel about themselves and their jobs is very important. Co-production should mean more power and resources being shared with people on the front line – people who use services, carers and frontline workers – so they are empowered to co-produce their own solutions to the difficulties they are best placed to know about. (Boyle and Harris, 2009; HSA and NDTI, 2009; Needham and Carr, 2009) 'Service users should be regarded as an asset encouraged to work alongside professionals as partners in the delivery of services' (Boyle and Harris, 2009, p 15).

What does personalisation mean for adult social care services?

> Personalisation is not a mechanism for public service reform.
> Rather, personalised services that meet the needs of the
> individual service user are one of the key objectives of such
> reforms. (Brooks, 2007, p 10)

This section discusses some of the emerging implications for:

- the social care workforce
- third sector organisations
- private sector providers
- user-led organisations
- commissioning
- regulation.

Finally the key issues for the social care sector as a whole are
summarised.

The social care workforce

> The social care workforce is not in a state of crisis or failure,
> but on the cusp of radical and comprehensive change at all
> levels. (Hudson and Henwood, 2009, p iv)

The role of social workers

Social work is seen by government as having a central role in
developing and delivering personalised social care and support
services (DH, 2009c; Hudson and Henwood, 2009). The authors of
Making it personal suggest that in a context of increasing self-
directed support, social work roles will adapt accordingly and

social workers could enjoy more creative, person-centred roles (Leadbeater and others, 2008). A statement affirming the role of social work for the delivery of Putting People First in England has been issued by ADASS, the Department of Health, Skills for Care, BASW and the Social Care Association (in conjunction with the Joint University Council Social Work Education Committee, SCIE and the GSCC). It clarifies the vital contribution of social work to personalisation, acknowledging it as an international, value-based profession. The statement sets out the purpose of social work and its distinct contributions, particularly those relating to better outcomes and increased control and independence for people who use services, their carers, families and wider community. It says 'social work is focused on supporting independence, promoting choice and control for people facing difficulties due to disability, mental health problems, effects of age and other circumstances' (Putting People First consortium, 2010c, p 1). Evidence shows that many still want the support of experienced social workers 'when they feel most vulnerable, to manage risks and benefits, and to build their self-esteem and aspirations so that they can take control or make difficult decisions' (ibid, p 2).

The key social work organisations involved make it clear that social work's distinct contribution is to make sure that services are personalised and that people's human rights are safeguarded through:

- building professional relationships and empowering people as individuals in their families and in communities, working through conflict and supporting people to manage their own risks
- knowing and applying legislation
- doing all of the above and also accessing practical support and services
- working with other professionals to achieve best outcomes for people.

Social workers bring together knowledge, skills and values and put these into practice, according to the experiences, relationships and social circumstances of the people they work with. Social workers therefore have a crucial role to play in multi-disciplinary teams because they can bring a perspective of the whole person, rather than focusing only on their symptoms, disability or circumstances: 'seeing the individual in the context of family, friends and community, and reflecting their hopes and fears for their own future is where social work can bring an important contribution to the work of the team' (ibid, p 2). Social work is regulated, graduate profession with a code of practice and a dynamic and evolving knowledge base. As personalisation develops existing social work skills can be strengthened and new ones developed to:

* support people with the assessment of their needs, circumstances and options
* work with families to improve well being and safeguard family members who may be in circumstances which make them vulnerable
* contribute to early intervention and preventative services, re-ablement, social inclusion, and helping to build capacity, social enterprise and social cohesion.

Social work and its values can potentially shape the responses to personalisation of the entire health and social care workforce. Listening, empowering individuals, recognizing and addressing potential conflict, safeguarding needs and the capacity of individuals, being sensitive to diversity and putting people in control should be central to the way staff and services treat people from the first point of contact. Social workers could have a leadership role here, particularly in the career structure proposed by the Social Work Task Force (see below), with advanced practitioners and consultant social workers.

The key social work bodies involved in drawing up the statement conclude that these are some of the areas that social work might develop into as personalisation progresses:

* Social work and interpersonal support – with the development of information, advice and advocacy services, support planning and brokerage, there may be new roles for social workers

alongside services led by people using services and their families. This may include services for people who fund their own social care.

- Social work and safeguarding rights – social work could have an important role in community development work and promoting social cohesion, for example where disabled, mentally ill or substance misusing people are victims of hate crime.
- Social work with families – social workers already help to break the cycle of families where generations of individuals are trapped in abusive relationships, crime, substance misuse, poor health, unemployment and other factors. Their role in this work could be strengthened to support the current priorities for local authorities to create safe, healthy and prosperous communities' (ibid, p 3).

People who use social work and care services and their carers consistently say:

> People value a social work approach based on challenging the broader barriers they face. They place a particular value on a social approach, the social work relationship, and the positive personal qualities they associate with their social worker. These include warmth, respect, being non-judgmental, listening, treating people with equality, being trustworthy, open, honest and reliable and communicating well. People value the support that social workers offer as well as their ability to help them access and deal with other services and agencies. (Shaping Our Lives, 2008)

Consistency and reliability have also been cited as especially important, along with the capacity for workers to keep their promises and go out of their way to help (Hopkins, 2007). The social work skills described here are those expected of social care practitioners in *Independence, well-being and choice*, which recognised that:

> people who use social care services say that the service is only as good as the person delivering it. They value social care

practitioners who have a combination of the right human qualities as well as the necessary knowledge and skills. If we are to deliver our vision this means workers who are open, honest, warm, empathetic and respectful, who treat people using services with equity, are non-judgemental and challenge unfair discrimination. The workforce is therefore critical to delivery. (DH, 2005a, p 14)

In statutory settings, some social work roles have sometimes become restricted by their 'gate-keeping' function and some social workers see personalisation as an opportunity to 'do real social work' with people, rather than be constrained by bureaucratic processes. But social workers will need to be empowered by their organisations to empower in turn the people who are using the services, so organisational issues need to be considered and changes implemented which enhance relationship-based frontline working. People who use social care and support services have recognised the limitations social workers can face when working within the constrained rules and resources of organisations (Beresford, 2007). One of the current roles for social workers is to ration resources and identify priorities. The need to manage resources is unlikely to go away even if many more people are

Photo: Photofusion

getting direct payments or have personal budgets (Blewett and others, 2007, p 25). While people who use services are clear that 'having a different relationship with social care staff is an important part of what they are seeking' (Blewett and others, 2007, p 28), they have been equally clear that the 'process of getting a service and the way in which it is delivered can have a major impact on users' experience of a service ... users did not perceive process as detached from outcome ...' (Shaping Our Lives and others, 2003, p 2). So people have indicated that although having greater choice of services may be a good thing, there also needs to be an improvement in how current services are provided, including addressing issues concerning budgets and rationing, along with the impact this has on the quality of social work. The National Consumer Council (NCC) recommends that 'where greater choice cannot create new efficiencies of scale or cost reduction, policy makers should be open and transparent about rationing decisions' (NCC, 2004, p 11).

Research is showing that frontline staff and firstline manager training and supervision is vital for the implementation of aspects of personalisation like personal budgets (particularly where people receive a direct payment), to manage change, improve knowledge and assessment practice, to promote equality and diversity awareness and to challenge perceptions about risk and capacity for certain groups (particularly older people and people with mental health problems or severe learning disabilities) who could benefit from the personal budget option (Carr and Robbins, 2009). One international research review option on different personal budget schemes said that 'social services practitioners who are not only well-informed, but also communicate that information to potential recipients and share their aspirations for independent living are important in helping people to maximize their opportunities for choice through cash-for-care schemes' (Arksey and Kemp, 2008, p 12). It is particularly important to target training at frontline staff who will be working directly with the person using the service and involved in the assessment and decision making processes, along with the person's carers (Ellis, 2007; Manthorpe et al, 2008a). Successful personal budget schemes are emphasising and facilitating frontline working with the same practitioner which is person-centred and relationship based, rather than that which focuses on processes and technical aspects in an environment with a high staff turnover (Barry, 2007; Schore and Foster, 2007; Arksey and Kemp, 2008; Bartlett, 2009; Carr and Robbins, 2009; Glendinning, 2009; NHS Confederation, 2009; Ottmann et al, 2009).

Social workers can also draw on their skills in counselling and community development to take forward personalisation. Here it is important to remember that personalisation is not only about personal budgets and self-directed support:

'There ... is a danger that assisting people with self-directed support could become the only and overriding definition of the social work role. Social work also has a contribution to make through its counselling competencies ... and has a tradition and track-record of community development, stimulating and supporting local community resources for disabled and older people' (Jones, 2008, p 46).

The final report of the Social Work Task Force, *Building a safe, confident future*, considers the context of personalisation in its recommendations for reform and recognises the need for:

- 'better training – with employers, educators and the profession all taking their full share of responsibility for investing in the next generation and in enabling social workers already in practice to develop their skills continuously
- improved working conditions – with employers signing up to new standards for the support and supervision of their frontline workforce that make good practice possible
- stronger leadership and independence – with the profession taking more control over its own standards, how it is understood and valued by the public, and the contribution it makes to changes in policy and practice
- a reliable supply of confident, high quality, adaptable professionals into the workforce, where they can build long-term careers on the frontline

- greater understanding among the general public, service users, other professionals and the media of the role and purpose of social work, the demands of the job and the contribution social workers make
- more use of research and continuing professional development to inform frontline practice'. (Social Work Task Force, 2009, p 2)

The government have accepted the Task Force's proposals for a social work career structure which allows experienced practitioners to progress in frontline roles as well as management; new standards for effective practice, supervision, manageable workloads and inter-disciplinary working; a new independent National College for Social Work; reforms to social work training and continuing professional development; a new licensing system and a probationary year (Burnham and Balls, 2009). The Ministers note the need to 'use social work skills and knowledge to take forward the personalisation agenda in adult social care' (ibid, p 6). Elsewhere other commentators have remarked that 'recruiting and retaining ... are important to the personalisation agenda because progress will be limited if there are insufficient workers with the right commitment, training and support to meet the unique needs of people who use social care services' (Hudson and Henwood, 2009, p ii).

Analysts have said that 'the challenges of workforce development and transformational change must be addressed in tandem' (Hudson and Henwood, 2009 p iv). In order to address the need for reaffirmation of some social work roles and for change in others, the Department of Health has produced an Adult Social Care Workforce Strategy which, as the Local Authority Circular states: 'recognises that in developing a more personalised approach, it is essential that frontline staff, managers and other members of the workforce recognise the value of these changes, are actively engaged in designing and developing how it happens, and have the skills to deliver it' (DH, 2008, p 8).

In the strategy document, *Working to put people first* (DH, 2009c), the Minister of State for Care Services said that the successful delivery of personalisation in adult social care depends on:

ensuring the development and support of a confident
and competent adult social care workforce Is now placed
centre stage. We need to give more support to the frontline
workforce – building on and recognising some of the amazing
work that is done... – in developing new skills and knowledge
to meet the challenges of the personalisation agenda. Our
agenda for equalities and human rights is fundamental to the
workforce as well as people using services. (ibid, p 1)

The Strategy was produced in consultation with stakeholders
and maps out six key priorities for the workforce to deliver
personalised services in the future:

- 'the leadership of local employers in workforce planning
  whether in the public, private or third sectors and of directors of
  Adult Social Services in their strategic commissioning role
- ensuring the right steps are taken to promote recruitment,
  retention, and career pathways to provide many of the
  workforce needs
- workforce remodelling and commissioning to achieve service
  transformation
- workforce development so we have the right people with the
  right skills; all to be in conjunction with
- more joint and integrated working between social, health care
  and other sectors; and
- regulation for quality in services as well as public assurance'.
  (ibid, p 3)

It also states the need for social work to support the major
cultural changes implied by the principles and values of
personalisation like choice and control; independent living; dignity
and respect; equal citizenship; good health and quality of life. This
means supporting the shift from:

- clients to citizens
- welfare to wellbeing
- expert to enabling
- transactional change to transformational change

- 'freedom from' to 'freedom to'
- safety net to spring board. (ibid, p 17)

The role of social care staff

Making the social care personalisation agenda a reality has implications not just for social workers but for all social care staff: 'Increasingly the workforce cannot be described simply in terms of local authority or independent sector, but must also include personal assistants, carers, volunteers, advocates and brokers' (Hudson and Henwood, 2009, p iv). The personalisation agenda will also influence the way health and other professionals (such as occupational therapists and nurses) work in multidisciplinary teams (for example community mental health teams). Increasingly people will make arrangements with private individuals to provide the support they need, and this will raise a range of issues about employment rights, pay, health and safety and safeguarding. This already applies to people who make their own private arrangements for care in their own homes without recourse to public funding.

The Skills for Care New Types of Worker programme is responding to some of these issues by exploring and developing what a new workforce will look like. The programme has been supporting pilot sites in England to explore workforce reform and trial new roles. In 2007 over 300 organisations took part in a mapping exercise which, among other things, identified personalisation as a key theme for workforce development. Skills for Care thinks new types of role might include:

- 'Hybrid roles' – this means, for example, social care workers or social workers doing tasks that have traditionally been done by other professionals such as workers from health, housing, justice, leisure, employment or other professions. It is any change to the way adult social care services are provided (or planned, commissioned or monitored) that aims to improve the lives of people using those services but is not yet available everywhere to everyone, or recognised as a 'mainstream' job, role or service.

- 'Person-centred working' – this means working in such a way that people who use services have as much control of their own lives as other people. This could be by making a person-centred plan or by using a direct payment or personal budget to arrange their own support and care, or to employ their own staff.
- 'Experts by experience' – people who have experience of using social care services or caring for people and who contribute to the 'business' of social care such as recruiting and training social care workers, assessing quality, commissioning services, planning changes to service delivery or regulation of services.
- Prevention and early intervention – workers supporting people early enough or in the right way, so that they don't need more intensive services. Types of provision might include support and modern equipment to stay at home, services provided in their community rather than in hospital, and support provided to keep people well and safe.
- Changes to organisations – to make them more effective, efficient and productive, for example, enabling workers to get their qualifications more quickly, working in partnership with other organisations and professions, integrating internally or externally or commissioning differently. (An example may be using the expertise that exists within user-led organisations to offer peer support to people planning their own care and support packages; or to offer experience-based advice and information).
- Community support – supporting community networks so that people can be independent from services. (Adapted from Skills for Care, 2007, pp 1–2)

Recent attention has been paid to those employed directly by individuals to fulfil the role of personal assistants (PAs). A Skills for Care-commissioned study of direct payment employers and personal assistants found that 79 per cent of direct payment users were very satisfied with the support they receive from their directly employed PA, compared with 26 per cent who had been very satisfied with services supplied directly by the local authority. The study also showed that 95 per cent of PAs 'love their work', 64 per cent were happy in their current role and many valued the flexible hours of the job (IFF Research, 2008). While this suggests that the direct payments system is working well for direct payment employers and PAs on an individual basis, the study also raises wider questions about the workforce such as pay, terms and conditions, training, registration and market capacity. These questions should be addressed ahead of the planned increase in strategic planning of personal budgets.

Photo: Careimages.com

The Skills for Care research also showed that one in three PAs considered themselves underpaid and that one in five thought they were required to work too many hours. The average hourly wage was found to be £7.60 an hour, with eight per cent of employers paying less than £6 an hour. (The UK national hourly minimum wage for adults over 22 was £5.80.) The research also found that 'the appropriateness and cost of training are an issue for direct payment employers, with only seven per cent of employers offering external training for PAs but a third of PAs wanting training and development for their role' (Skills for Care, 2008, p 1). These findings echo some concerns about the fact that PAs and homecare agency staff can work in conditions where they have little access to training, guaranteed holiday and sick pay, pensions or collective bargaining. It has been argued that people employing workers using direct payments (or personal budgets) 'need to be able to offer reasonable terms and conditions of employment to attract employees, and these workers deserve to be paid a fair wage' (Leece, 2007, p 195) so that 'user-controlled support does not founder on the inability of users to recruit and retain their personal assistants' (p 194).

Many other workers providing homecare support are employed by third sector or private agencies, which may have less favourable terms and conditions than the public sector (DH and Department for Education and Skills, 2006). The majority of those working in this sector are female, there are an increasing number of migrant workers in the field and staff turnover can be high (Experian, 2007; Eborall and Griffiths, 2008). Private sector employers argue that the pay and conditions of service they can offer their staff are constrained by what is affordable within the contract price set by public commissioners, and that policy expectations will not be delivered unless providers are funded realistically (ECCA, 2008).

Those planning, purchasing and providing personalised social care services need to be aware of the potential wider impact of certain associated workforce developments: 'Increasing user-controlled support may result in women losing jobs in the public sector where they have pension provision, union representation and safe working environments for casual employment as personal assistants with less beneficial terms and conditions' (Leece, 2007, p 194).

The Trades Union Congress (TUC) Commission on Vulnerable Employment's remit includes people who work for social care agencies or in care homes as being at risk of 'vulnerable employment' – that is, in precarious work where there may be an imbalance of power in the employer–worker relationship. The Commission warns that In certain low-paid sectors such as care, some employers may routinely break employment law and recommend that 'responsible employers should work together to challenge vulnerable employment' (TUC, 2008, p 5).

A report published by the Commission for Rural Communities says that 'the personalisation of social care will also have an effect on the social care workforce ... as many participants observed. Some were optimistic that new employment opportunities would emerge and saw this as a way to sustain local economies and communities. Others foresaw greater instability and disadvantages for care workers. Local authorities need to manage these risks with partner organisations and local needs assessments' (Manthorpe and Stephens, 2008, p 37). Workers with experience of working with older people in some rural budget pilot sites say they are concerned about travelling to remote areas, and the often isolated nature of their work (Manthorpe and Stephens, 2008).

Practice example: Independent living
Sense East's supported living project, Norfolk

A young woman who is deaf-blind and has a complex syndrome with a deteriorating effect on both her mobility and intellect was identified as needing support by the outreach team. Her home life was becoming isolated and her ageing parents were struggling to cope.

A supported living project was set up to enable the young woman to live independently in the community. The complex care team consulted her and her parents about what sort of housing would best suit her needs and preferences. The young woman decided on a town location and wanted a one-bedroom ground-floor flat with no garden. The young woman, her parents and Sense then explored what level of support she needed and how this would take place, and a funding package was set with the local authority. The package was awarded to Sense with the full support of the young woman and her family.

The young woman then participated in the selection of her team and they supported her in equipping the flat, with parental input as she directed. She has a personal finance plan and is involved in planning her daytime activities. Her evening funding is such that she has a staff team to take her anywhere she chooses.

At a strategic level, the Department of Health have said that 'the personalisation agenda will entail more sophisticated workforce planning which makes explicit links with other sectors. Such workforce planning must maximise opportunities for strategic market development, bring together skills across different professional groups, identify different ways of working and spell out the changing requirements within professional roles' (DH, 2008c, p 18).

Skills for Care and Skills for Health have indicated some of the different ways of working for PAs in their seven Common Core Principles for Self Care. These principles can be used to help people develop practical solutions to working as a PA.

The principles are:

1   ensure individuals are able to make informed choices to manage their self-care needs
2   communicate effectively to enable individuals to assess their needs, and develop and gain confidence to self-care
3   support and enable individuals to access appropriate information to manage their self-care needs
4   support and enable individuals to develop skills in self-care
5   support and enable individuals to use technology to support self-care
6   advise individuals how to access support networks and participate in the planning, development and evaluation of services
7   support and enable risk management and risk taking to maximise independence and choice (Skills for Care/Skills for Health 2008).

The principles were developed in partnership with people who use services and carers. PAs can use the principles to work with the person they are supporting, develop job descriptions and to agree individual learning plans.

For home care workers personalisation means rethinking some of their traditional task-centred personal care role. This could include a wider range of support such as domestic help, household management and correspondence, home maintenance and gardening or even being taken out. Care workers could be trained by agencies to widen their support skills (Sawyer, 2008).

The Social Policy Research Unit (SPRU) found that personalisation, particularly personal budgets, offers 'new opportunities for [home care] agencies, including opening up new markets and demands for new types of support, such as help with shopping and social activities' (Baxter et al, 2008, p 1). Skills for Health have looked at new professional career development and progression opportunities for independent care home staff to provide new levels of personalised care. This is being designed to enhance staff flexibility, aims at reducing staff turnover and improving continuity of care and relationships with the people living in the care homes as well as their families and carers (Skills for Health, 2008).

The role of social work and social care leaders and managers

It has been noted that 'the transformation agenda has direct implications for leadership and management. The new vision demands additional skills and competencies from commissioners, managers and senior leaders. Transforming leaders will be expected to create the conditions for others to transform realities, to galvanise innovators and to inspire, communicate and operationalise the new vision' (Hudson and Henwood, 2009, pii). The Adult Social Care Workforce Strategy is very clear about the need for good leadership, effective management and commissioning skills so that change is well facilitated and services can be transformed: 'New cadres of leadership talent need to be planned and fostered in both the independent and public sectors. User-led organisations and networks will grow and provide strong voices ... Directors of Adult Social Services (have) a pivotal role in leading workforce change locally through their responsibility for strategic workforce commissioning, working with local employers' (DH, 2009c, p 5). The Strategy outlines the need for new types of leadership at all level, including the front line, and says that leaders need to:

• 'look to people who use services and their communities
• be skilled at collaboration across systems and boundaries
• work well within complex systems
• be developed at all levels of the organisation
• keep in direct contact with frontline services as their careers develop'. (ibid, p 22)

In a report on leadership for personalisation and social inclusion in mental health by leaders in the field of mental health social work, the authors say 'leadership challenges include driving a values-led service and systems transformation, whole-system workforce reform and a need for sustained and cultural change within and across organisations' (Allen, Gilbert and Onyett, 2009, p vi). The sort of leadership needed to bring about the type of transformation needed for personalisation is seen as very different from the managerial, 'command and control' model, focused on one person at the top:

> 'strategic, operational and grassroots leadership for personalisation is most likely to be grounded in relationship building, the development of shared values across systems, the encouragement of creativity, the capacity to influence others and 'hosting' and facilitating collective inputs and energies rather than 'directing' them. Modest but robust confidence and strong ethics – rather than thrusting heroic styles – may become more important in public services, with an emphasis upon the enablement of others. The importance of pursuing human rights, sound ethics and equalities will grow through this agenda... Leadership may need to be a more dispersed activity than hitherto, founded on widely shared, common goals and values amongst many stakeholders and emerging out of new cross-organisational cultures and including more visible 'citizen leaders'. Leaders and leadership will need to be developed in new ways if the benefits of personalisation are to be realised. Different people within the system will need to be offered opportunities to develop their confidence and skills.' (ibid, p vi)

The National Skills Academy for Social Care, which supports training, development and career support in adult social care for England, is developing a leadership and management programme to strengthen the workforce in this area (National Skills Academy for Social Care, 2009) and Skills for Care have produced some principles of workforce redesign for leads and managers. After research and consultation, Skills for Care distilled seven principles for workforce redesign to address the challenges and ensure the changes that the personalisation agenda brings:

1 take a whole systems view of organisational change
2 recognise how people, organisations and partnerships respond differently to change
3 nurture champions, innovators and leaders
4 engage people in the process – acknowledge and value their experience
5 be aware of the ways adults learn
6 change minds and change systems
7 develop workforce strategies that support transformation and recognise the shape of resources available in the local community. (Thomas and Balman, 2008)

In addition, Skills for Care have published some adult social care manager induction standards, which reflect the new skills and professional environment needed for personalisation and social care transformation. The standards 'are based on management practice which has person-centred planning at its heart' and mean that managers should 'support independence' and 'treat people with respect and dignity and support them in overcoming barriers

Photo: Photofusion

to social inclusion ... (including) the most disadvantaged groups'
(Skills for Care/Skills for Business, 2008). The standards are as
follows:

1 understanding the importance of promoting social care
   principles and values – these underpin good leadership
2 providing direction and facilitating change – including
   understanding role, responsibility, accountability and the social
   and environmental contexts in which the organisation operates
3 working with people – developing team and individual
   performance through good supervision, recruitment and
   induction, training and communication
4 using resources – understanding responsibilities for finance,
   contracts, buildings and technology
5 achieving outcomes – delivering a quality, person-centred
   service and understanding responsibility for partnership
   working, information sharing and change management
6 managing self and personal skills – taking responsibility
   for continuing professional development, leadership and
   management skills.

Third sector organisations

The term 'third sector' is used to describe organisations that:

* are independent of the government
* work to achieve social, environmental and cultural aims
* mainly reinvest any profits they make to achieve those social,
  environmental or cultural aims.

The sector includes community groups, co-operatives and mutuals,
voluntary groups, charities and social enterprises. (Adapted from
HM Treasury, 2007, p 1)
   Building on progress states that 'the government should support
the development of the many new and innovative services that
provide tailored advice to specific community interest groups'
(Prime Minister's Strategy Unit, 2007, p 42) and Putting People
First makes it clear that a crucial part of developing personalised

services is supporting third sector innovation, including social enterprise. *Independence, well-being and choice* says that 'local partners will need to recognise the diversity of their local population and ensure that there is a range of services, which meet the needs of all members of the local community' (DH, 2005a, p 12). In 2007 the Treasury issued its plans for the future role of the third sector in social and economic regeneration (HM Treasury, 2007), which stress the need for capacity-building and investment in the long-term future of the sector, which is seen as vital to transforming public services. This includes the development of 'micro markets' of very small providers and user-led organisations

Practice example: Personalisation in a residential setting
Anchor Homes' food ordering system

Anchor Homes is the largest not-for-profit provider of residential and nursing care for older people. In 2006 they began piloting a new meal ordering system in their care homes. Previously residents had to order their food a day or more in advance, as was the case in most care homes. However, under the new system residents are able to choose what they want as they sit down to eat. Now they can choose based on seeing and smelling the food.

This more personalised approach to mealtimes means that staff don't have to spend hours collecting food orders in advance and are freer to provide care and support. Now residents are making decisions based on what they like the look and smell of, they are eating more and less is wasted. Any savings go back into buying even better food.

Residents are more adventurous in their food choices. The chefs regularly hold meetings and gather feedback from residents on meal choices and are guided by residents' requests and favourite recipes. If what's on offer doesn't appeal to someone, chef managers can still make a simple alternative if that's what the individual would prefer.

(ULOs), which offer peer support, information, advocacy and advice as well as sometimes providing services (NAAPS/DH, 2009b; DH, 2010b).

Clearly the third sector has a key part to play in the personalisation of social care services, having the potential to offer a wider choice of specific or specialist services, particularly for people from minority groups who have been historically underserved by generic statutory agencies: 'We recognise the role of third-sector organisations in representing the voices of different groups and campaigning to achieve change for individuals and communities' (HM Treasury, 2007, p 2). Strategic engagement with this sector in social care may help to address some of the issues with service provision and local diversity in certain areas (Harlock, 2009). The government is particularly keen to encourage the growth of third sector providers as 'markets can challenge inefficiency – but the 'm' word raises fears of commercialisation and profit in services funded by the taxpayer for some of society's most vulnerable people. A community business that reinvests its surplus largely or entirely back into the business (and therefore the community) overcomes many such qualms' (Lorimer, 2008, p 1).

The Association of Chief Executives of Voluntary Organisation (ACEVO) Commission on Personalisation is looking at how to radically shape new social markets across all main public service areas, including social care: 'We propose social markets that exist within a new legal framework of roles, rights and responsibilities – a new social contract' (ACEVO, 2009, p 5). It has outlined five key building blocks for the future:

- Devolving financial control: control over how money is spent on the services should be devolved down to a level as close as possible to the service user.
- Self-help and mutual aid [co-production]: the service-centric model of 'public services' should be turned inside-out, with self-help and mutual aid (in other words, community) placed firmly at its heart. We should see people not as 'service users' but as 'service helpers' and change agents.
- Building 'can do' assets: personalisation should inspire a revolution on the supply side of public services, a revolution

that sees far-reaching culture change throughout the system, that frees up public service professionals and that creates an environment in which innovation flourishes.
* Social markets: a new generation of genuine social markets should be created, in which power shifts from commissioner and provider to service users, and in which good performance is rewarded and invested in and poor performance is driven out (Adapted from ACEVO, 2009, p 5).

A social enterprise has been defined as 'a business that reinvests its surplus primarily back into the business for the interest of the community rather than working to make a profit for the benefit of shareholders alone' (Lorimer, 2008, p 12). The third sector, of which social enterprise is a part, is seen as important for delivering the diversity of provision to support the scope and type of choice required by the personalisation agenda. Local Area Agreements (LAAs) can be used to enable strategic planning and service delivery with the third sector and other community partners: 'Here, working with the third sector as a partner in the delivery of public sector services is a valuable approach, bringing with it flexibility, diversity and the potential to add value through contacts with additional revenue sources and increasing the social capital of communities. Many third sector organisations locally will also be uniquely placed to better support the hard-to-engage and disadvantaged groups within a community' (p 8). Such third sector partners should, for example, include user-led organisations. The National Council of Voluntary Organisations (NCVO) has been very clear about the important role the third sector has to play not only in providing unique, personalised services for individuals, but in building local and community resources for the benefit and well-being of all. It asserts that 'operating at the frontline, VCOs [voluntary and community organisations] are often highly aware of local need and can identify gaps in provision and meet the short falls' (Harlock, 2009, p 7).

One particular area of provision that has the potential to be delivered through social enterprise is brokerage, information and advocacy services for people using personal budgets or direct payments: 'Personalisation support services facilitated

Photo: Photofusion

by social enterprise are a valuable area for consideration, while commissioners may take longer to establish agreed strategic needs that will drive the shape of a wider, mixed economy of care' (Lorimer, 2008, p 16). The Department of Health and key partners in the social care transformation agenda have said that access to information, advice and advocacy is essential for all adults who need social care and support (together with their carers, families and friends). They recognise the role of the third sector in providing this essential service infrastructure, particularly user-led organisations (IDeA, 2009a).

A Demos study has suggested that there will be positive impacts for the third sector from the increased use of personal budgets in social care, particularly as much of the innovation, advocacy and campaigning which resulted in the current wider social care reform had its roots in the work of social enterprise and voluntary organisations such as user-led Centres for Independent Living (Bartlett and Leadbeater, 2008). However, the authors warn that as the social care market develops, traditional third sector organisations will need to be mindful of the need to adapt and compete: 'Although the third sector has the right value base to thrive in a world of personal budgets, they might not always be as good at competing in the market – which may require branding, marketing and customer relationship management – as private sector providers' (p 5).

NCVO have outlined some of the key roles for third sector organisations in taking personalisation forward:

- building user-focused and responsive services that reflect the needs and wishes of local people
- developing a skilled and person-centred workforce able to respond flexibly to user needs and preferences
- adapting systems and processes to meet the requirements of micro-commissioning and purchasing through self-directed funding mechanisms
- helping users understand and access information on services available and plan for their support
- working with commissioners to give a voice to service users' need and shape the provision of personalised services (Harlock, 2009, p 9).

Private sector providers

Nearly half of all adult social care staff are employed by the private and voluntary sector and in many places they provide the majority of most services (CSCI, 2008a). Owners, managers and staff in the private sector thus have a crucial role to play in developing personalised solutions to people who use their services.

When direct payments were implemented, the Department of Health suggested that 'the greater use of direct payments and individualised budgets have the power to destabilise existing care markets' (DH, 2005b, p 27). Independent sector providers are becoming increasingly aware of this reality as the personalisation agenda is beginning to transform the way social care services are being conceived, commissioned and delivered. An increase in the use of self-directed support and personal budgets means there will be a smaller role for lengthy block-contracting and in-house service provision.

More generally, local authorities and partners will be looking to purchase different types of service from different sorts of provider.

The aim is to foster greater choice and more flexible, responsive services to provide a more personalised service in both community and residential settings. It is likely that the projected changes are most likely to affect residential care home providers, day centres and domiciliary support services. However, there will almost certainly be a growth in the market for personal assistants and small-scale, flexible, specialist providers (Leece, 2007; Bartlett and Leadbeater, 2008; Sawyer, 2008) and for extra care or supported housing, particularly for older people (Housing21, 2008; Sitra, 2009).

For people in need of care and support, choice is only possible if the services they want to purchase are readily available, of good quality and have spare capacity to respond to choice. Local markets in many areas, particularly rural areas, still provide only limited choice to people. In the case of residential care, the increasing dominance in the market of a relatively small number of large corporate providers means that being given a personal budget may be of little significance, as the consumer has an increasingly limited choice of provider (Dittrich, 2008). Thus local authorities have been asked to develop and shape the market to ensure sufficient provision for enabling choice. This means reforming how services are commissioned and procured (Bennett, 2008). There is also a question of 'how to ensure that greater choice for users stimulates innovation and quality in what providers deliver, rather than increasing financial risk to a level where they cease to be viable, potentially leading to the contraction of the market (and therefore of choice)' (Sitra, 2009, p 8).

To develop services that are focused on the person, and are competitive within a social care market geared towards personalisation, private sector (and other) providers can learn from what their customers (including older people living in residential care or nursing home settings) are saying and what the personalisation policy seeks to achieve. As Bartlett and Leadbeater note: 'While the private sector care services offer more flexible hours, its services can also be too impersonal. Care depends on intimacy and relationships – it is not just a transaction, but a relationship of trust between carer and cared for. The contracted-out care services market often fails to deliver such relationships, for example it has a very high staff turnover, which it consistently complains about' (Bartlett and Leadbeater, 2008, p 18). So private providers need to ask whether they are able to respond to the demand for individually tailored services based on good, stable relationships between staff and people using services. Many of the issues relevant to personalised services in care homes are being explored through the work of the My Home Life (MHL) programme (Owen and NCHRDF, 2006). Through an extensive literature review the programme has found that quality of life for older people in care homes can be captured by the following themes:

- managing transitions
- maintaining identity
- creating community
- shared decision making
- improving health and health care
- supporting good end-of-life care
- keeping the workforce fit for purpose
- promoting a positive culture.

The work of the MHL programme in developing resources and a practice network to support care homes has its focus on the quality of life of people living in care homes. The personalised care and support necessary to put this into routine practice means seeing the 'community' of a care home consisting of those visiting and working there as well as residents. The English Community Care Association (ECCA) has produced a case-study based 'route map' to the delivery of personalised care for independent sector providers of both residential and community based care and support services for all people who use social care (ECCA, 2010).

Equally, local authorities should work with providers to help with predicting how the market might change and to encourage innovation (Manthorpe and Stephens, 2008). A new, more trusting relationship is required between commissioner and provider. This should be based on achieving the right outcomes for the individual, their carers and community rather than financial concerns: 'at present service providers are kept at arm's length from the detailed planning process, because they are perceived as tending to drive up costs in order to meet their own needs' (Bartlett and Leadbeater, 2008, p 28). However, it has been recommended that 'dialogue between providers and commissioners must always reflect and be driven by what is best in the interests of people and communities' (Harlock, 2009, p 12).

The concerns of many providers that personalisation and other policy expectations will not be delivered unless accompanied by realistic public funding have already been noted.

User-led organisations

It is important to recognise that personalisation is not about individual solutions *per se* but represents a broader, more varied approach. The potential for personalisation to encompass collective ways of working has been articulated by Iain Ferguson:

> A sense of powerlessness ... affects not only those who use health and social services, but also those who work in them. Overcoming that sense of powerlessness, however, will involve moving beyond individualism and the market-based solutions of personalisation theory. It will require the development and strengthening of *collective* organisation both amongst those who use services and amongst those who provide them. One of the most exciting and challenging developments in social work and social care over the past twenty years – Independent Living Centres [sic], advocacy schemes, new models of crisis services and, above all, social models of disability and mental health – have emerged out of the collective experience and organisation of service users. (Ferguson, 2007, p 401)

In relation to discussion about personalisation, individualism and community, it has been noted that 'it must be recognised that service users are not isolated individuals but are part of a larger community or public. This collectivism is crucial to the concept and nature of public services, which must meet and balance both the collective needs of the community and those of individuals' (Harlock, 2009, p 6). Service users themselves consistently emphasise the need for collective user-led and peer support organisations based on the fundamental principles of 'the social model of disability and the philosophy of independent living developed by service users themselves' (Beresford and Hasler, 2009, p 56).

> **Practice example: A user-led organisation**
> *Essex Coalition of Disabled People*
>
> Essex Coalition of Disabled People (ECDP) is an organisation run by and for disabled people, including people with mental health problems. Established in 1995, its origins are firmly rooted in a belief that the voice of disabled people, both as individuals and collectively, is vital.
>
> ECDP's vision is to enhance the everyday lives of disabled people in Essex and beyond. It does this in a variety of ways. For example, ECDP provides a wide range of support, information, advice and guidance services – providing direct payment and personal budget support services to just over 3,500 people. A new independent support planning service run by ECDP enables people to have choice and control over their care and support, with everyone who uses this service taking some form of cash payment. ECDP also provides a range of disability equality-based training for individuals and organisations in the public, private and voluntary sector, alongside a CRB administrative service that processed over 500 CRBs from February 2009 to February 2010.
>
> In total, ECDP has over 1,500 members and just under 70 volunteers all of whom are closely engaged with ECDP to ensure its work, and so the work of public bodies, is based on the lived experience and voice of disabled people.
>
> More details about ECDP can be found on their website: www.ecdp.org.uk.

Some have argued that highly individualised approaches may undermine collective social care initiatives and opportunities for developing cooperative organisations led by those using services, or peer advocacy. One report concerning the implementation of self-directed support and personal budgets identified the loss of collectivism 'where there is an apparent tension between the emphasis on the individual rather than on collective objectives' (Henwood and Grove, 2006, p ii) as an ideological obstacle to reform. The Institute for Public Policy Research (IPPR) has stated that individual choice is best supported by 'having forms of collective voice and influence, peer support and accountability of providers to users ... [but] routes for collective influence are currently lacking, as are spaces in which to engage with and support each other' (Moullin, 2008, p 5), while the New Economics Foundation (nef) argues that 'personal budgets without mutual support misunderstand the nature of public services' (nef, 2008, p 15). Similarly, the National Council for Voluntary Organisations has asserted that 'user-led initiatives and mutual organisations can offer users more market power by jointly commissioning and managing services. They can also ... promote networks of support which are essential to wellbeing' (Harlock, 2009, p 6).

Photo: Photofusion

IPPR has recommended that 'mechanisms for exercising collective voice should be focused on larger and more significant decisions and priority-setting exercises, and be better resourced' (Brooks, 2007, p 9). Putting People First makes it clear that as part of system-wide transformation there should be 'support for at least one local user led organisation and mainstream mechanisms to develop networks which ensure people using services and their families have a collective voice, influencing policy and provision' (HM Government, 2007, p 4). As part of this commitment the government has published an advisory document *Putting people first: Working together with user-led organisations* (HM Government, 2009b) in partnership with people who use services and others, which outlines the benefits that local authorities and their residents enjoy when they work with user-led organisations. These benefits range from helping local authorities deliver greater personalisation to improved engagement with seldom-heard population groups.

The Improving the Life Chances of Disabled People strategy of 2005 (Prime Minister's Strategy Unit, 2005) included the expansion of centres for independent living to support, advise and advocate for disabled people. The direct involvement of disabled people through centres for independent living was seen as one of the key ingredients to the Life Chances programme and is now understood as a vital component of wider social care transformation. The National Centre for Independent Living (NCIL) and the Association of Directors of Adult Social Services (ADASS) have a joint protocol for the provision of centres for independent living and user-led support services (NCIL/ADASS, 2006).

There is an expectation that councils will talk directly to disabled people and their organisations in order to implement system change, but this assumes that those user-led organisations exist and have the capacity to undertake their new and expanded roles. In 2006 the Department of Health commissioned a research study into the role and capacity of user-led organisations. The national mapping exercise showed that 'the existence of local user-led organisations is inconsistent and patchy. In some areas (18 localities or 12 per cent) no user-led organisations were identified at all, while in a substantial number only one to five

user-led organisations were found (76 localities or 51 per cent)'
(Maynard Campbell, 2007, p 5). Since 2007 only 22 per cent of
local authorities have engaged user or carer led organisations in
the delivery of support to all service user groups, while only 18 per
cent had extended user-led organisational support to self-funders
(ADASS, 2009a). Further development work is therefore needed
if user-led organisations are to have as powerful and influential a
role as they should.

However, some key principles have been learned from early
activity around developing individual and community capacity to
support people to self-direct:

* grow your own co-production networks by building a local
  community of interest with people using services, carers and
  their organisations
* councils and user and carer led organisations need to be
  proactive in building partnerships around personalisation and
  the Social Care Reform Grant can be used for this
* co-production doesn't just happen and needs leadership and
  investment
* small steps can make big changes and investing in user and
  carer support groups can build trust
* people feel empowered to learn and use support planning skills
  themselves (DH 2010b, pp 4–5).

The cross-government Independent Living Strategy (Office of
Disability Issues, 2008) includes an investment in the development
of 12 user-led organisations as action and learning sites to
promote service improvement, mentoring between organisations
and to share learning to foster the development of user-led
organisations in general. However, it will be up to local authorities
to support user-led organisations as partners because 'the success
of [the] whole system change is predicated on engagement with
communities and their ownership of the agenda at local level'
(DH, 2008a, p 9). A critical success factor for user-led organisation
development 'appeared to be how user-led organisations are
perceived and supported within the local authority environment;
such as where they fit in to local spending priorities; whether

the idea of nurturing a strong user voice is seen as important or "difficult"; or whether it is down to one or two individuals who have reason to champion the cause' (Maynard Campbell, 2007, p 8). As part of their personalisation strategies, local authorities will need to commit to resourcing user-led organisations and to recognise them as equal partners in Local Area Agreements rather than optional extra or tokenistic consultants (Bennett, 2008): 'The value of services provided by service user organisations needs to be written into service level agreements. If services are run by service user organisations they could bring health and social care together' (Shaping Our Lives and others, 2007, p 13).

The Department of Health have made it clear that by 2011 all 152 councils will be expected to have made significant steps towards redesign and reshaping their adult social care services (in the light of their JSNAs) with the following in place: 'An enabling framework to ensure people can exercise choice and control with accessible advocacy, peer support and brokerage systems with strong links to user led organisations. Where user led organisations do not exist, a strategy to foster, stimulate and develop these locally.' (DH, 2009d, p 5)

Commissioning

Commissioning was defined by the former Commission for Social Care Inspection (CSCI) (now part of the Care Quality Commission) as 'the process of translating aspirations into timely and quality services for users which meet their needs; promote their independence; provide choice; are cost effective; and support the whole community' (CSCI, 2006, p 5). The vision for NHS world-class commissioning states that the activity is more about transformation than transaction (DH, 2007a) and the NHS Institute for Innovation and Improvement (NHS Institute) has issued a guide for health and social care commissioners designed to promote service innovation (NHS Institute, 2008). Lord Darzi's NHS review recommendations also include World Class Commissioning (WCC), which incorporates eleven competencies to improve PCT commissioner capacity to work jointly with local authorities and other partnership outside the NHS. The

WCC programme 'aims to deliver a more strategic and long-term approach to commissioning services, with a clear focus on delivering improved health outcomes and better value for money. It has been developed jointly by the DH and the wider health and care community and will be delivered locally by the NHS' (Audit Commission, 2009, p 59). Lord Darzi's *NHS next stage review final report* says also that 'every primary care trust will commission comprehensive wellbeing and prevention services, in partnership

---

Practice example: Strategic commissioning
'Sustainable commissioning' in Camden

The Camden commissioning project, which has been funded through the Treasury 'Invest to Save' budget, aims to improve the way public services are commissioned so that the wider social, economic and environmental impacts of services are taken into account. The project is piloting the New Economics Foundation's Sustainable Commissioning Model to look again at the provision of day services for people with mental health problems. The winner of the tender to provide new day services in mental health was a consortium of local organisations including MIND in Camden, Holy Cross Centre Trust and Camden Volunteer Bureau. The consortium was not the cheapest tender on a unit cost basis, but commissioners felt their focus on wider social and economic impacts would create the most positive outcome for the whole community.

The Sustainable Commissioning Model contains two key elements:
1. An **Outcomes Framework** to ensure social, economic and environmental impacts are accounted for in the tendering process and delivery. The framework encourages innovation by allowing providers to explain how their activities and outputs will achieve certain service level and wider outcomes, as identified by the local authority.
2. A **Valuing Model** which tracks social, environmental and economic outcomes and includes a financial savings component. (www.procurementcupboard.org)

with local authorities, with services offered personalised to meet the specific needs of their local populations' (DH, 2008d, p 9). This approach is already underpinned by joint strategic needs assessments, where primary care trusts and local authorities are expected to produce strategies for the health and wellbeing of their local community.

The NHS is calling for more joint commissioning between primary care trusts (PCTs) and local authorities, as evidence shows that too much PCT commissioning may take place without integrating with local authority social care: 'A greater focus on joint commissioning between healthcare and social care and better integration between healthcare, social care and other local government services will bring benefits for patients and service users' (Bell, 2010).

Health and social care partners do not always know about the joint financing options available as part of joint commissioning. The Audit Commission has provided guidance to local authorities and the NHS to support the move away from concentrating on the mechanics of joint financing and the processes of partnership and instead look at how joint funding and closer integration can improve people's lives. They argue that agreed outcomes should be the focus of joint working to help older people and those who need mental health and learning disability services. Pooling funds can improve services for people using services, but often the actual financial arrangements can become the focus of attention: 'Organisations can usually describe how they now work better together but often not how they have jointly improved user experience' (Audit Commission, 2009, p 4). The Audit Commission emphasise that:

> 'NHS and social care organisations increasingly need to work together in partnership to get better value from available resources and improve services and outcomes for users. There are many different approaches and mechanisms available for joint financing, but the focus should always be on value for money and improving the user experience' (ibid, 2009, p 5).

However, in the context of personalisation in social care, the Audit Commission note that because NHS services are free at the point of use and social care is subject to means as well as needs testing 'pooled funds may need to be separated to allow personal budgets for social care' (ibid, p 34). It is likely that this issue will be explored in the personal health budget pilots.

Greater partnership working between all public services will also be supported by the Audit Commission's Comprehensive Area Assessment (CAA) framework and Oneplace approach. The CAA is designed to 'strengthen the ability of people to influence how services are provided and improved' (Audit Commission, 2009, p 5).

Oneplace is the online interface for CAA reporting so that people can see how well their local authorities are performing. When the Department of Health looked at emerging practice on 'contracting for personalised outcomes', it found that:

A common feature underpinning the changes in each council has been a shift from traditional and often adversarial relationships towards collaborative and constructive partnerships between commissioners and providers. (Bennett and Miller, 2009, p 4)

Following *Putting people first* (HM Government, 2007), by 2011 all councils will be expected to have:

a commissioning strategy which includes incentives to stimulate development of high quality services that treat people with dignity and maximise choice and control as well as balancing investment in prevention, early intervention/reablement and providing intensive care and support for those with high-level complex needs. This should have the capacity to support third/private sector innovation, including social enterprise and where appropriate undertaken jointly with the NHS and other statutory agencies such as the Learning and Skills Council. (DH, 2008a, p 24)

It is clear that local authorities have been tasked with 'shaping and building the market' to make sure people have a choice of services.

Local authorities are now being encouraged to change from thinking about service commissioning to thinking about strategic investment: 'Directors of adult social services will need to consider making some long term investments in innovative services that users are starting to request.... Commissioners need to become what some have termed "strategic bridge builders" meaning they look for gaps in the market for services people seem to be demanding and use strategic investments to encourage this market to develop' (Bartlett and Leadbeater, 2008, p 29). One important area is to sustain and stimulate local 'micro-markets' and to remove barriers which make it hard for innovative and highly personalised micro social care and support enterprise to develop (NAAPS/DH, 2009a). As part of a drive towards better use of adult social care resources, local authorities have been encouraged to invest in preventative and reablement services as part of the personalisation and transformation agenda (Bolton, 2009).

The notion that commissioning needs to change if personalisation is to become a reality has been strongly stressed (CSCI, 2006; Bennett, 2008; ACEVO, 2009; Bartlett, 2009; Harlock, 2009) and directions on how this might be achieved are gradually emerging. In its framework for commissioning, the former CSIP stressed the need for a balance between a focus on market-shaping and other commissioning issues relating to personal budgets and building on the broader agenda of commissioning for the health and wellbeing of all citizens so that the benefits of personalisation can be felt by everyone: 'All people are dependent on social networks, universal services and the resources of communities in which they live to become active citizens. This logically leads to the consideration of an inclusive approach to commissioning – that is about shaping the places in which we live and supporting everyone to live better lives' (Bennett, 2008, p 13). The former CSIP offered a model of multi-level commissioning that includes:

- Strategic commissioning – area-wide and regional-level joint commissioning with a three- to ten-year outlook. Working across whole community to develop the local market to support personalisation, to develop the workforce and to ensure that universal public services are accessible to all.

- Operational commissioning – locality-based commissioning and support to citizens commissioning. Day-to-day commissioning activities with a one- to two-year outlook. Working to support citizens in directing their own care with information, advocacy, brokerage and training.
- Citizen commissioning – citizens directing their own support, personal budget holders.

As noted earlier, to enable successful commissioning for personalisation, 'the traditional split of interests between providers and commissioners must end. Information about market trends, gaps and difficulties must be shared ... this means sharing information about ... strategy and direction, spending decisions, commissioning vision and market intelligence' (Bartlett, 2009, p 35).

In order to gather and use the type of person-centred information needed to inform and drive commissioning, the Department of Health has outlined a simple six-stage process, based on the principles of co-production, which should be carried out at least every year:

1 gathering the person-centred information – eg from individual outcome-focused reviews
2 transferring the information into a usable format – capturing the top three things that are working and not working in people's lives and the three things they feel are most important for the future
3 clustering the information into three themes
4 analysing the information
5 action planning
6 sharing information (Bennett and Sanderson, 2009).

The Institute of Public Care (IPC) has explored the move commissioning needs to make from focusing on outputs to outcomes for personalisation and says that 'the need is to shift the debate about outcomes from a method of defining strategic goals to one where it defines the practical relationships between service users, commissioners and providers' (IPC, 2009, p 9).

Regulation

Overview

The shift towards person-centred services raises questions about the role and functions of regulatory bodies and systems. Social care has inherited a regulation and inspection system which is focused more on the services rather than the person using them, their carers and families. A regulation and inspection system needs to ensure that policies and procedures provide assurance around quality and safety, as well as focus on better outcomes for people (Fraser, 2008). A new regulatory framework for health and adult social care which focuses on quality and safety is to be implemented by the Care Quality Commission (CQC) from April 2010: 'For the first time, it will create a common framework for providers from all sectors (public, private, third sector) and across healthcare and adult social care. For people who use services it will provide greater assurance of the safety and quality of services, and offer them better information on which to make their choice of service provider.' (DH, 2009e, p 1). The proposed regulations aim to put the service user or patient at the centre of standards and decision making, with the inclusion of an explicit requirement to respect and involve service users. The CQC describes a new system that is consistent with the personalisation agenda:

> The new registration system for health and adult social care will make sure that people can expect services to meet essential standards of quality and safety that respect their dignity and protect their rights. The new system is focused on outcomes rather than systems and processes, and places the views and experiences of people who use services at its centre. (CQC, 2009, p 6)

The new regulations are clear that 'agencies that directly provide personal care (for example domiciliary care agencies), or those that have a continuing role in the personal care of an individual (for example, introduction agencies who might monitor carers' performance, respond to complaints, or develop care plans) will need to register with the Care Quality Commission' (DH, 2009e, p 12). However, if someone chose to be supported by family or friends then, 'where such care was wholly under the control of the person receiving it, this would not require registration' (DH, 2009e, p 22). The details of the draft regulations have been set out in The Health and Social Care Act 2008.

Personalisation requires new, more flexible approaches to regulation, able to adapt to innovative support from new types of providers offering broader opportunities including scope for people to take appropriate risks. It will also be important to establish close working links between the regulator and the Director of Adult Social Services, given the latter's remit for commissioning, market development and quality assurance, as well as local adult protection services. It has been noted that, in the context of personalisation and the transformation of adult social care 'modern regulation must find an approach which is consistent with promoting choice and control while also offering appropriate safeguards' (Hudson and Henwood, 2009, p iii). Research on micro providers (that is, very small social care and support services of five staff or less) has shown that applying disproportionate regulation and legislation designed for large scale providers is a barrier to developing and sustaining very small scale initiatives which are often flexible and innovative, based on models of co-production and rooted in the local community (NAAPS/DH, 2009a).

The former CSCI (now part of CQC) responded to the challenges of personalisation by starting its Experts by Experience inspection programme, where people who use services have a direct role as inspectors. The Commission's assessment of council services in 2007/08 took into account the Putting People First agenda, considering how personalisation policies were being applied in communities. The assessments included new performance measures and inspection methods appropriate to personalisation (CSCI, 2008b). The Care Quality Commission (CQC) is implementing person-centred regulatory approaches, intended to empower the people who use services, their carers and families. Their guidance on direct payment support schemes outlines which services will need to be registered, and this clarifies some of the confusion about this aspect of personalisation, including support brokerage schemes requiring registration status as domiciliary care agencies (CQC, 2008). The CQC regulatory approach also includes standards on levels of choice and control, to strengthen personalisation and person-centred care and support.

Workforce regulation

The General Social Care Council (GSCC) is assessing if there is support for the regulation of personal assistants (PAs). The key principles that will shape their approach are:

- any register must add value to the experience of people employing their own PAs
- it must enable people to make informed choices when employing a PA who is a friend or family member
- the form of regulation must fit with the new freedoms and flexibilities granted to people under the personalisation agenda. (Adapted from GSCC, 2008b.)

Safeguarding is an aspect of regulation that is of concern to social care stakeholders implementing approaches to service delivery that increase choice and control. The initial findings from the individual budget (IB) pilot site evaluation concluded that local authority adult protection leads can have unique insights from working at the intersection between the demand for safety for the individual, assurances about spending public money and the increased demand for choice and control in social care. The researchers recommend that their expertise is used consistently with IB implementation, with safeguarding issues being addressed at an early stage (Manthorpe and others, 2008b).

The former CSCI recognised that 'it is important not to be over-protective or prevent adults from leading ordinary lives – but this must be weighed against individuals' fundamental right to expect to be safe and to be protected and safeguarded from harm' (CSCI, 2008c, p 11). It emphasised the need for clarity for roles and responsibilities of agencies involved in safeguarding adults (within social care and wider public services) with clearer definitions of what constitutes abuse and harm. The Department of Health's *Independence, choice and risk: A guide to best practice in supported decision-making* recognises the complexities involved in managing risk in relation to choice. However, the guide is clear that 'ultimately, the local authority has a statutory duty of care and a responsibility not to agree to support a care plan if there are serious concerns that it will not meet an individual's needs or if it places an individual in a dangerous situation' (DH, 2007b, p 2).

Practice example: Information and advice
Brighton and Hove Access Point

The Access Point is the adult social care contact centre for Brighton and Hove. It provides a point of access for adults wishing to access social care services or who require advice and information in order to access services independently.

The Access Point brings together the Older People's Community Assessment team, the Physical Disability (under 65) Assessment team, the Sensory team, Occupational Therapy and the Learning Disability team. By contacting the centre by phone, minicom, e-mail or fax, the person using the service can access information on or assessment for any one or more of these services. Traditionally each of these services had its own contact number and would complete its own initial assessment, meaning that people who required more than one service or advice and information from a variety of services would need to call various numbers and undergo a number of assessments. The Access Point ensures more accessible services, and needs- as opposed to service-led assessment.

What are the key issues for the social care sector as a whole?

The personalisation vision set out in *Putting people first: A shared vision and commitment to the transformation of adult social care* (HM Government, 2007) is underpinned by four key themes, as illustrated in the figure below. These key themes are discussed further in the document called *Putting people first: The whole story*, which came with the 2009 Local Authority Circular on Transforming Adult Social Care (DH, 2009d).

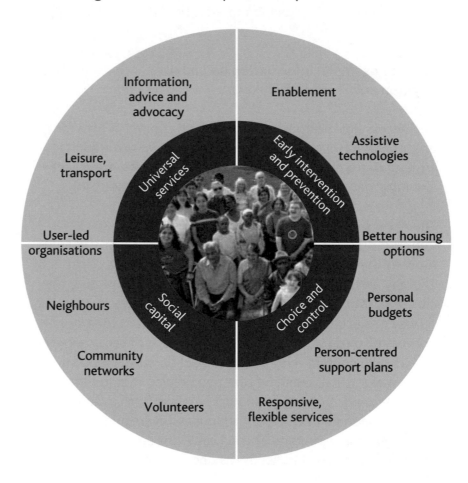

In their report *From safety net to springboard*, the Equality and Human Rights Commission produced a series of seven broad principles to guide social care transformation. The principles are:

1 'care and support based on clear outcomes and founded on human rights and equality
2 access to publicly funded care and support based on clear, fair and consistent criteria
3 individuals and their families in control of their care and support
4 the right balance between safety and risk to promote choice and independence
5 local strategic partnerships that play a central role in developing and maintaining local care and support
6 funding that balances affordability and sustainability with fairness
7 equality and human rights law and practice re-calibrated to respond to our ageing society' (EHRC, 2009, pp 6-7).

Transformation milestones for local authorities

In spring 2009, the Association of Directors of Adult Social Services (ADASS) and the Local Government Association (LGA) surveyed council progress in delivering Putting People First. Following this, in September 2009 ADASS and the LGA, supported by the Department of Health, published a series of milestones to help councils check that they are delivering transformed services and support.

The five key priorities for achieving personalisation and transformation in adult social care by spring 2011 are that:

- the transformation of adult social care, has been developed in partnership with people who use services (both public and private), their carers and other people who are interested in these services
- a process is in place to make sure that all those eligible for council-funded adult social care support will receive a personal

budget via a suitable assessment process (usually self-directed support)
- partners are investing in cost-effective preventative interventions which reduce the demand for social care and health services
- everyone has access to information and advice regarding how to identify and access options available in their communities to meet their care and support needs
- people who use services are experiencing increased choice and improvement in quality of care and support service supply, built upon involvement of key stakeholders (councils, primary care trusts, people who use services, providers, third sector organisations and so on), who can meet the aspirations of all local people (whether council- or self-funded) wanting to obtain social care services (Putting People First consortium, 2009; IDeA, 2009b).

Social care service transformation will be supported by:

- joint strategic needs assessments (JSNAs) which inform and underpin joint strategic commissioning strategies that are responsive to local need and focused on outcomes
- management and development of the social care market to ensure a choice of high-quality, flexible and responsive services for people purchasing their own care directly or through self-directed support and personal budgets
- national and regional systems in place to support the implementation of the adult social care personalisation agenda through the Putting People First transformation programme (DH/IDeA, 2009).

The personalised system will need to be cost-effective, sustainable in the long term and consistent with the principles of fairness and universalism. Personalised care and support is one of the fundamental pillars of the new National Care Service, with choice and control being one of the founding principles (HM Government, 2010).

4

Conclusion

Person-centred support is not another thing services have to
do; it's what they must do. It's not another job – it's *the* job
(Glynn and others, 2008, p 11).

Personalisation means thinking about public services and social
care in an entirely different way – starting with the person
rather than the service. Although this shift will take time, it will
ultimately mean change at every level throughout the whole
local authority system to ensure that universal services such as
transport, housing and education are accessible to all citizens. This
means that commissioning must change to be more strategic and
open, with a focus on the local community, its resources and the
people who use the services. Approaches to early intervention and
prevention need to develop further so that people are encouraged
to stay healthy and independent.

In social care, system-wide organisational and cultural change
will need to take place so that people, rather than systems and
procedures, come first. This will include fostering innovative
and collaborative ways of working, giving universal access to
information and advice to everyone in need of support regardless
of where their funding comes from. It will also require supporting
social care practitioners to work in new ways alongside people
who use services, their carers, families and communities. New
models of leadership will need to develop to drive and respond to
the fundamental changes in power sharing and the renewed focus
on frontline relationships.

This guide is intended to sketch out our current understanding
of personalisation. SCIE is supporting the sector by rapidly
absorbing lessons from innovations and pilots, drawing on the
experiences of creative implementers and emerging research
findings, and making these accessible through further products
and initiatives.

Further information

For more on personalisation

The Social Care Institute for Excellence
www.scie.org.uk

SCIE has co-produced a series of At a glance Personalisation briefings looking more closely at implications for different social care stakeholders:

At a glance 06: Personalisation briefing: Implications for commissioners
At a glance 07: Personalisation briefing: Implications for home care providers
At a glance 08: Personalisation briefing: Implications for housing providers
At a glance 10: Personalisation briefing: Implications for carers
At a glance 12: Personalisation briefing: Implications for advocacy workers
At a glance 13: Personalisation briefing: Implications for voluntary sector service providers
At a glance 14: Personalisation briefing: Implications for personal assistants (PAs)
At a glance 15: Personalisation briefing: Implications for user-led organisations (ULOs)
At a glance 17: Personalisation briefing: Implications for residential care homes
At a glance 18: Personalisation briefing: Implications for community mental health services
At a glance 20: Personalisation briefing: Implications for nursing homes

At a glance 21: Personalisation briefing: Implications for people with autistic spectrum conditions and their family carers
At a glance 22: Personalisation briefing: Implications for community learning disability staff

Other useful SCIE resources on personalisation

Social Care TV www.scie.org.uk/socialcaretv with films and related interactive resources. Film titles include:

What is personalisation?
Personalisation for older people: living at home
Personalisation for older people: supported housing
Personalisation for older people: residential care
Personalisation for someone with a learning disability
Personalisation for someone with a physical disability
Personalisation and mental health

Personalisation e-learning resources: www.scie.org.uk/publications/elearning

For more information on how direct payments work please see SCIE's *Resource Guide 5: Direct payments: answering Frequently Asked Questions*, which was produced with the National Centre for Independent Living (NCIL).

For more information on how direct payments are working for black and minority ethnic people please see SCIE's *Race equality Position Paper 1: Will community-based support services make direct payments a viable option for black and minority ethnic service users and carers?*

For more about the role of people who use services in culture change see *SCIE People management Knowledge Review 17: Developing social care: service users driving culture change*, produced by Shaping Our Lives, National Centre for Independent Living and University of Leeds Centre for Disability Studies, and *SCIE At a glance 4: Changing social care.*

For further background information on personal budgets
Glasby, J. and Littlechild, R. (2009) *Direct payments and personal budgets: Putting personalisation into practice*, Bristol: The Policy Press.

Social Care Online
www.scie-socialcareonline.org.uk

Department of Health personalisation web pages
www.dh.gov.uk/en/SocialCare/Socialcarereform/Personalisation/index.htm

Transforming Adult Social Care (TASC)
www.tasc.org.uk/

in Control
www.in-control.org.uk

My Home Life
www.myhomelife.org.uk/

The IBSEN project – National Evaluation of the Individual Budgets Pilot Projects
http://php.york.ac.uk/inst/spru/research/summs/ibsen.php

DH Care Networks

Network gateway
www.dhcarenetworks.org.uk

Personalisation
www.dhcarenetworks.org.uk/Personalisation

DH Care Networks Personalisation toolkit
www.dhcarenetworks.org.uk/Personalisation/Topics

For general information on social care transformation

Care Quality Commission (CQC)
www.cqc.org.uk

General Social Care Council (GSCC)
www.gscc.org.uk

Skills for Care
www.skillsforcare.org.uk

New Types of Worker
www.newtypesofworker.co.uk

National Skills Academy for Social Care
www.nsasocialcare.co.uk

Skills for Health
www.skillsforhealth.org.uk

Office for Disability Issues
www.officefordisability.gov.uk

Office of the Third Sector
www.cabinetoffice.gov.uk/third_sector.aspx

Improvement and Development Agency for local government (IDeA)
www.idea.gov.uk

Local Government Association
www.lga.gov.uk

Association of Directors of Adult Social Services (ADASS)
www.adass.org.uk

British Association of Social Workers (BASW)
www.basw.co.uk

Shaping Our Lives National User Network
www.shapingourlives.org.uk

National Centre for Independent Living (NCIL)
www.ncil.org.uk

National Council for Voluntary Organisations (NCVO)
www.ncvo-vol.org.uk

Association of Directors of Voluntary Organisations (ACEVO
www.acevo.org.uk

Demos
www.demos.co.uk

English Community Care Association (ECCA)
www.ecca.org.uk

National Care Association (NCA)
www.nationalcareassociation.org.uk

Chartered Institute of Public Finance and Accountancy (CIPFA)
www.cipfa.org.uk

National Mental Health Development Unit 'Paths to Personalisation' resource
www.pathstopersonalisation.org.uk

References

ACEVO (2009) *Making it personal: A social market revolution – The interim report of the Commission on Personalisation*, London: ACEVO.

ADASS (2009a) *Making progress with Putting people first: Self-directed support*, London: DH/ADASS/IDeA/LGA

ADASS (2009b) *Putting people first: Measuring progress*, London: ADASS/LGA.

ADASS (2009c) *Personalisation and the law: Implementing Putting people first in the current legal framework*, London: DH/ADASS.

ADASS (2009d) *Common resource allocation framework*, London: DH/ADASS.

Allen, R., Gilbert, .P and Onyett, S. (2009) *SCIE Report 27: Leadership for personalisation and social inclusion in mental health*, London: Social Care Institute for Excellence.

Arksey, H. and Kemp, P. (2008) *Dimensions of choice: A narrative review of cash-for-care schemes*, Working Paper No DHP 2250, York: SPRU, University of York.

Audit Commission (2009a) *Comprehensive area assessment: A guide to the new framework*, London: Audit Commission.

Audit Commission (2009b) *Means to an end: Joint financing across health and social care*, London: Audit Commission.

Barry, M. (2007) *Effective approaches to risk assessment in social work: An international literature review*, Edinburgh: Scottish Executive Social Research.

Bartlett, J. (2009) *At your service: Navigating the future market in health and social care*, London: DEMOS.

Bartlett, J. and Leadbeater, C. (2008) *Personal budgets: The impact on the third sector*, London: Demos.

BASW (British Association of Social Workers) (2002) *The code of ethics for social work*, Birmingham: BASW.

Baxter, K., Glendinning, C., Clarke, S. and Greener, I. (2008) *Domiciliary care agency responses to increased use choice*, York: SPRU, University of York.

Bell, L. (2010) *NHS Evidence – commissioning briefing 09/02/10*, London: NHS Evidence (www.library.nhs.uk/commissioning/ViewResource.aspx?resID=282410).

Bennett, M. (2008) *Commissioning for personalisation: A framework for local authority commissioners*, London: Care Services Improvement Partnership/DH.

Bennett, S. and Miller, C. (2009) *Contracting for personalised outcomes: Learning from emerging practice*, London: DH.

Bennett, S. and Sanderson, H. (2009) *Working together for change: Using person-centred information for commissioning*, London: DH.

Bennett, T., Cattermole, M. and Sanderson, H. (2009) *Outcome-focused reviews – A practical guide,* London: DH.

Beresford, P. (2007) *The changing roles and tasks of social work from service users' perspectives: A literature-informed discussion paper*, London: Shaping Our Lives National User Network.

Beresford, P. and Hasler, F. (2009) *Transforming social care: Changing the future together*, London: Brunel University Press.

Blewett, J., Lewis, J. and Tunstill, J. (2007) *The changing roles and tasks of social work: A literature-informed discussion paper*, London: General Social Care Council.

Bolton, J. (2009) *Use of resources in adult social care: A guide for local authorities*, London: DH.

Boyle, D., Clark, S. and Burns, S. (2006) *Co-production by people outside paid employment*, York: Joseph Rowntree Foundation.

Boyle, D. and Harris, M. (2009) *The Challenge of Co-production: How equal partnerships between professionals and the public are crucial to improving public services*, London: NESTA.

Brooks, R. (ed) (2007) *Public services at the crossroads: Executive summary*, London: Institute for Public Policy Research.

Burnham, A. and Balls, E. (2009) *Government response to the Social Work Task Force*, London: DCSF/DH.

Carr, S. and Robbins, D. (2009) *SCIE Research Briefing 20: The implementation of individual budget schemes in adult social care*, London: SCIE.

Challis, D. and others (2007) *Individual budgets evaluation: A summary of early findings*, York: University of York Social Policy Research Unit, available at www.york.ac.uk/inst/spru/pubs/rworks/IbsenSummary.pdf

CQC (Care Quality Commission) (2008) *Direct payment support schemes: Information for service providers on which services need to be registered*, London: CQC (www.cqc.org.uk/guidanceforprofessionals/socialcare/careproviders/guidance.cfm?widCall1=customWidgets.content_view_1&cit_id=2595).

CQC (2009) *Essential standards of quality and safety*, London: CQC.

CQC (2010) *The state of health care and adult social care in England: Key themes and quality of service in 2009*, London: CQC.

CSCI (Commission for Social Care Inspection) (2006) *Relentless optimism: Creative commissioning for personalised care*, London, CSCI.

CSCI (2008a) *State of social care in England 2006–2007*, London: CSCI.

CSCI (2008b) *CSCI Annual report 2007–2008*, London: The Stationery Office.

CSCI (2008c) *Raising voices: Views on safeguarding adults*, London: CSCI.

Department for Communities and Local Government (2006) *Strong and prosperous communities*, London: HMSO.

DH (Department of Health) (2001) *Valuing people: A new strategy for learning disability for the 21st century*, London: The Stationery Office.

DH (2005a) *Independence, well-being and choice: Our vision for the future of social care for adults in England*, London: DH.

DH (2005b) *Health reform in England: Update and next steps*, London: DH.

DH (2006) *Our health, our care, our say: A new direction for community services*, London: DH.

DH (2007a) *World class commissioning: Vision*, London: DH.

DH (2007b) *Independence, choice and risk: A guide to best practice in supported decision-making – Executive summary*, London: DH.

DH (2008a) *Local authority circular LAC (DH)(2008)1: Transforming social care*, London: DH.

DH (2008b) *The future regulation of health and adult social care in England: A consultation on the framework for the registration of health and adult social care providers*, London: DH.

DH (2008c) *Putting people first – working to make it happen: Adult social care workforce strategy – interim statement*, London: DH.

DH (2008d) *High quality care for all: NHS next stage review final report*, London: DH

DH (2009a) *NHS Personal health budgets update (December 2009)*, London: DH.

DH (2009b) *Understanding personal health budgets*, London: DH.

DH (2009c) *Working to Put People First: The strategy for the adult social care workforce in England*, London: DH.

DH (2009d) *LAC (DH) (2009) 1: Transforming adult social care*, London: DH.

DH (2009e) *Response to the consultation on draft Regulations for the framework for the registration of health and adult social care providers*, London: DH.

DH (2009f) *Safeguarding adults: Response to consultation on the review of the No Secrets guidance*, London: DH.

DH (2010a) *Putting people first: Personal budgets for older people – making it happen*, London: DH.

DH (2010b) *Putting people first: Planning together – peer support and self-directed support*, London: DH.

DH and Department for Education and Skills (2006) *Options for excellence: Building the social care workforce of the future*, London: DH.

DH/IDeA (2009) *Transforming adult social care delivery support architecture*, London: LGA.

Dittrich, R. (2008) *Putting people first briefing paper 7: The care market – summary of pre-existing evidence from experts and research*, available at http://www3.hants.gov.uk/briefingpaper7-2.pdf

Duffy, S. (2008) *in Control mythbuster and frequently asked questions*, Birmingham: in Control publications.

DWP (2008) *Raising expectations and increasing support: Reforming welfare for the future*, London: The Stationery Office.

Eborall, C. and Griffiths, R. (2008) *The state of the adult social care workforce in England 2008: The third report of Skills for Care's skills research and intelligence unit*, Leeds: Skills for Care.

ECCA (English Community Care Association) (2008) *Nothing for services, nothing for quality*, London: ECCA.

ECCA (2010) *Personalising Care: A route map to delivery for care providers*, London: ECCA.

EHRC (Equality and Human Rights Commission) (2009) *From safety net to springboard: A new approach to care and support for all based on equality and human rights*, London: EHRC.

Ellis, K. (2007) 'Direct payments and social work practice: the significance of "street-level bureaucracy" in determining eligibility', *British Journal of Social Work*, vol 37, no 3, pp 405–22.

Experian (2007) *Overseas workers in the UK social care, children and young people sector: A report for Skills for Care and Development*, London: Skills for Care and Development.

Ferguson, I. (2007) 'Increasing user choice or privatising risk? The antimonies of personalisation', *British Journal of Social Work*, vol 37, pp 387–403.

Fraser, J. (2008) *Personalisation and regulation*, CSCI presentation to SCIE independent sector seminar on personalisation 15 July 2008, unpublished.

Glendinning, C. et al (2008) *The national evaluation of the Individual Budgets pilot programme*, York: SPRU, University of York.

Glendinning, C. (2009) *Combining choice, quality and equity in social services: Synthesis report – Denmark*, Brussels: European Commission on Employment, Social Affairs and Equal Opportunities.

Glynn, M. and others (2008) *Person-centred support: What service users and practitioners say*, York: Joseph Rowntree Foundation.

GSCC (General Social Care Council) (2008a) *Social work at its best: A statement of social work roles and tasks for the 21st Century*, London: GSCC.

GSCC (2008b) *Media release 30/06/08: Consultation announced on the regulation of personal assistants*, London: GSCC.

Harlock, J. (2009) *Personalisation: Rhetoric to reality*, London: NCVO

Henwood, M. and Grove, B. (2006) *Here to stay? Self-directed support: Aspiration and implementation – A review for the Department of Health*, Towcester: Melanie Henwood Associates.

HM Government (2007) *Putting people first: A shared vision and commitment to the transformation of adult social care*, London: HM Government.

HM Government (2008) *Carers at the heart of 21st century families and communities: A caring system on your side, A life of your own,* London: HM Government.

HM Government (2009b) *Putting people first: Working together with user-led organisations,* London: DH.

HM Government (2010) *Building the National Care Service,* London: The Stationery Office.

HM Treasury (2007) *The future role of the third sector in social and economic regeneration,* London: Cabinet Office.

Hopkins, A. (2007) *Delivering public services: A report to the Office of the Third Sector by the National Consumer Council,* London: National Consumer Council.

Housing21 (2008) *'Building choices': Personal budgets and older people's housing – broadening the debate: Report,* London: Housing Corporation/CSIP.

HSA & NDTI (2009) *A guide to co-production with older people,* Christchurch: National Development Team for Inclusion.

Hudson, B. and Henwood, M. (2009) *Working for people: The workforce implications of Putting people first – A report for the Department of Health,* Towcester: Melanie Henwood Associates.

IDeA (Improvement and Development Agency for local government) (2009a) *Transforming adult social care: Access to information, advice and advocacy,* London: IDeA/DH/LGA.

IDeA (2009b) *10 questions to ask if you are scrutinising the transformation of adult social care,* London: IDeA/CfPS.

IFF Research (2008) *Employment aspects and workforce implications of direct payment,* Leeds: Skills for Care.

IPC (2009) *Changing the currency of commissioning from outputs to outcomes,* Oxford: Oxford Brookes University.

Jones, R. (2008) 'Self-directed support: watching for the pitfalls', *Journal of Integrated Care,* vol 16, no 1, pp 44–7.

Leadbeater, C. (2004a) *A summary of 'Personalisation through participation: A new script for public services',* London: Demos.

Leadbeater, C. (2004b) *Personalisation through participation: A new script for public services,* London: Demos.

Leadbeater, C., Bartlett, J. and Gallagher, N. (2008) *Making it personal,* London: Demos.

Leece, J. (2007) 'Direct payments and user-controlled support: the challenges for social care commissioning', *Practice*, vol 19, no 3, pp 185–98.

Lorimer, R. (2008) *Integration for social enterprise*, London: CSIP Integrated Care Network.

Lyons, M. (2007) *Lyons inquiry into local government: Place shaping – a shared ambition for the future of local government*, London: The Stationery Office.

Manthorpe, J. and Stephens, M. (2008) *The personalisation of adult social care in rural areas*, Cheltenham: Commission for Rural Communities.

Manthorpe, J. et al (2008a) 'Training for change: early days of individual budgets and the implications for social work and care management practice: a qualitative study of the views of trainers', *British Journal of Social Work*, (advance access, 7 March 2008), pp 1-15.

Manthorpe, J. and others (2008b) 'Safeguarding and system change: early perceptions of the implications for adult protection services of the English individual budgets pilots: a qualitative study', *British Journal of Social Work*, Advance Access, 17 March 2008.

Maynard Campbell, S. (2007) *Mapping the capacity and potential for user-led organisations in England*, London: DH.

Moullin, S. (2008) *Just care? A fresh approach to adult services*, London: Institute for Public Policy Research.

NAAPS/Department of Health (2009a) *Supporting micromarket development: Key messages for local authorities*, London: DH.

NAAPS/DH (2009b) *Supporting micromarket development: A concise, practical guide for local authorities*, London: DH.

National Skills Academy for Social Care (2009) *Leadership and management prospectus*, London: National Skills Academy for Social Care.

NCC (National Consumer Council) (2004) *Making public services personal*, London: NCC.

NCIL/ADASS (2006) *Joint protocol between National Centre for Independent Living (NCIL) and Association of Directors of Social Services (ADASS) for the provision of Centres for Independent Living (CILs) and user-led support services*, London: NCIL/ADASS.

Needham, C. and Carr, S. (2009) *SCIE Research Briefing 31: Co-production: an emerging evidence base for adult social care transformation*, London: SCIE.

nef (new economics foundation) (2008) *Co-production: A manifesto for growing the core economy*, London: nef.

NHS Confederation (2009) *Shaping personal health budgets – A view from the top*, London: The NHS Confederation.

NHS Confederation (2009a) *Personal health budgets – The shape of things to come?*, London: The NHS Confederation.

NHS Confederation (2009b) *Shaping personal health budgets – A view from the top*, London: The NHS Confederation.

NHS Institute for Innovation and Improvement (2008) *Commissioning to make a bigger difference: A guide for NHS and social care commissioners on promoting service innovation*, London: DH.

ODI (Office for Disability Issues) (2009a) *Government response to the consultation on the Right to Control*, London: ODI

ODI (2009b) *Right to Control: Prospectus for potential Trailblazers*, London: ODI

Office for Disability Issues (2008) *Independent living: A cross-government strategy about independent living for disabled people*, London: HM Government Office for Disability Issues.

Owen, T. and NCHRDF (2006) *My home life: quality of life in care outcomes*, London: Help the Aged.

Poll, C. and Duffy, S. (eds) (2008) *A report on in Control's second phase: Evaluation and learning 2005–2007*, London: in Control publications, available at www.in-control.org.uk/dynamic_download/in_download_389.pdf

Poll, C. and others (2006) *A report on in Control's first phase 2003–2005*, London: in Control publications, available at www.library.nhs.uk/learningdisabilities/viewResource.aspx?resID=187216

Prime Minister's Strategy Unit (2005) *Improving the life chances of disabled people*, London: Cabinet Office.

Prime Minister's Strategy Unit (2007) *HM Government policy review: Building on progress: Public services*, London: HM Government.

Putting People First consortium (Department of Health) (2009) *Making progress with putting people first: NCAS conference briefing*, London: Putting People First consortium/IDeA/LGA/SCIE.

Putting People First consortium (2010a) *Advice note (January 2010): Personal budgets: Council commissioned services*, London: DH.

Putting People First consortium (2010b) *Briefing note (January 2010): Personal budgets: Managed services*, London: DH.

Putting People First consortium (2010c) *The future of social work in adult social services in England: Statement,* London: Putting People First consortium.

Sawyer, L. (2008) 'The personalisation agenda: threats and opportunities for domiciliary care providers', *Journal of Care Services Management*, vol 3, no 1, pp 41–63.

Shaping Our Lives (2008) in General Social Care Council *Social work at its best: A statement of social work roles and tasks for the 21st century*, London: General Social Care Council.

Shaping Our Lives National User Network and others (2003) *Shaping our lives – from outset to outcome,* York: Joseph Rowntree Foundation.

Shaping Our Lives, National Centre for Independent Living and University of Leeds Centre for Disability Studies (2007) *SCIE people management knowledge review 17: Developing social care: Service users driving culture change*, London: SCIE.

Sitra (2009) *Personalisation, prevention and partnership: transforming housing and supported living*, London: Sitra/CLG.

Skills for Care (2007) *New type of worker/working*, available at www.skillsforcare.org.uk/view.asp?id=894

Skills for Care (2008) *News Release 30/06/08: Skills for Care launches first major study of direct payment employers and personal assistants*, Leeds: Skills for Care.

Skills for Care/Skills for Health (2008) *Common core principles to support self care*, Leeds/Bristol: Skills for Care/Skills for Health.

Taylor, J. and others (2007) *We are not stupid*, London: Shaping Our Lives and People First Lambeth.

TUC (Trades Union Congress) (2008) *Hard work, hidden lives: The short report on the commission on vulnerable employment*, London: TUC.

Image: 'Personalisation in social care – some history and context' by Pen Mendonca penmendonca@btinternet.com